The Humanitarian-Development-Peace Nexus Interim Progress Review

OECD

This work is published under the responsibility of the Secretary-General of the OECD. The opinions expressed and arguments employed herein do not necessarily reflect the official views of the Member countries of the OECD.

This document, as well as any data and map included herein, are without prejudice to the status of or sovereignty over any territory, to the delimitation of international frontiers and boundaries and to the name of any territory, city or area.

The statistical data for Israel are supplied by and under the responsibility of the relevant Israeli authorities. The use of such data by the OECD is without prejudice to the status of the Golan Heights, East Jerusalem and Israeli settlements in the West Bank under the terms of international law.

Note by Turkey
The information in this document with reference to "Cyprus" relates to the southern part of the Island. There is no single authority representing both Turkish and Greek Cypriot people on the Island. Turkey recognises the Turkish Republic of Northern Cyprus (TRNC). Until a lasting and equitable solution is found within the context of the United Nations, Turkey shall preserve its position concerning the "Cyprus issue".

Note by all the European Union Member States of the OECD and the European Union
The Republic of Cyprus is recognised by all members of the United Nations with the exception of Turkey. The information in this document relates to the area under the effective control of the Government of the Republic of Cyprus.

Please cite this publication as:
OECD (2022), *The Humanitarian-Development-Peace Nexus Interim Progress Review*, OECD Publishing, Paris, https://doi.org/10.1787/2f620ca5-en.

ISBN 978-92-64-42049-6 (print)
ISBN 978-92-64-48663-8 (pdf)
ISBN 978-92-64-93198-5 (HTML)
ISBN 978-92-64-52130-8 (epub)

Preface

2022 marks the mid-point of the Sustainable Development Goals (SDGs). The SDGs were designed to be an ambitious but achievable "blueprint to achieve a better and more sustainable future for all".

Multiple, overlapping crises – climate crisis, COVID-19 and conflict – are undermining progress across all SDGs. In some cases, progress on development is in reverse, plunging millions of people back below the poverty line. This is particularly true in places affected by fragility and conflict.

Before the pandemic, an estimated 80% of people living in extreme poverty would be living in fragile countries and regions in 2030. The pandemic has made things worse, exacerbating underlying causes of conflict and fragility. Climate change is a risk multiplier, making natural disasters more frequent and heightening food and livelihood insecurity for hundreds of millions.

New conflicts in previously stable countries and regions are creating additional and acute humanitarian needs. More food insecurity in developing countries will be one of the most severe legacies of the conflict in Ukraine. Even before the Ukraine crisis, United Nations (UN) Office for the Coordination of Humanitarian Affairs (OCHA) estimated that humanitarian needs were at record levels, with 274 million people needing humanitarian assistance in 2022.

As needs have grown, funding for humanitarian and development activities has struggled to keep pace. Official Development Assistance from members of the Development Assistance Committee rose to record levels in 2021 – USD 179 billion – but needs continue to outstrip available resources. The international community needs to ensure that its actions in support of humanitarian and development goals are as efficient and effective as possible.

There is room for improvement. Too often, we work in siloes (humanitarian – development – peace) and fail to talk to each other and agree on joint plans and programmes. And yet, all this work is funded by the same donors. Rigid thinking reduces the international community's ability to support fragile countries and people and we must do better.

The DAC Recommendation on the Humanitarian-Development-Peace Nexus was born out of a recognition of the need to rethink traditional ways of working. It is the result of intensive consultations involving a broad coalition of countries, UN entities, funds and programmes and civil society.

As this report shows, the DAC Nexus Recommendation provides a useful common framework for more effective international engagement in fragile and conflict affected places. Three years after its adoption, we are seeing some good progress. Stubborn challenges remain, but we are convinced that the principle of improved coordination and collaboration between bilateral and multilateral actors is an essential part of the recovery from the world's current crises. We encourage all actors in fragile and conflict affected states and regions to place the nexus approach at the core of their work, with the urgency that these multiple crises demand.

Susanna Moorehead
Chair,
Development Assistance Committee

Foreword

In February 2019, the OECD Development Assistance Committee (DAC) adopted its Recommendation on the Humanitarian-Development-Peace Nexus and tasked the International Network on Conflict and Fragility (INCAF) with overseeing its operationalisation. This interim report, presented in advance of the monitoring report due in 2024, is a preliminary stocktaking exercise for the purpose of joint learning and as input for future events, including the high-level follow-up Partnership for Peace roundtable in May 2022. It analyses DAC and United Nations (UN) adherents' efforts to align with the principles of the DAC Recommendation.

The aim of this report is to take stock of achievements and lessons so far, and feed the ongoing collective reflection on how to put the nexus approach into practice. It is not intended as a full assessment of adherents' progress against the objectives of the DAC Recommendation: this will be part of the formal monitoring report in 2024.

This study contains both qualitative and quantitative data from a variety of primary and secondary sources. A global survey of DAC members, UN adherents, and their national government and civil society counterparts in host partner countries generated critical quantitative data and written comments. This Nexus Interim Report Survey was distributed to target specific profiles at headquarters and country level. A review of reports, policies and evaluations of the efforts by DAC and UN adherents and their partners further informs the study. OECD statistics on official development assistance (ODA) flows to fragile and conflict-affected settings were also used in this exercise. Several networks of actors involved in the nexus approach were consulted, among them the Inter-Agency Standing Committee Results Group 4, the Peace and Security Thematic Working Group of the DAC-Civil Society Organisations (CSO) Reference Group, and the DAC-UN Dialogue.

While comprehensive, it should be acknowledged that this report was researched and written within the limitations of available data, resources and time.

Acknowledgements

This interim stocktaking report was prepared by the Organisation for Economic Co-operation and Development (OECD) under the auspices of the International Network on Conflict and Fragility (INCAF) and in consultation with the group of United Nations (UN) adherents to the DAC Recommendation on the Humanitarian-Development-Peace Nexus. The OECD would like to thank the many contributors for their engagement throughout the process.

This report would not have been possible without the contributions of the DAC and UN adherents to the DAC Recommendation, who helped distribute the Nexus Interim Report Survey, and of participating development, humanitarian and peace partners. In particular, the drafting team would like to thank the many colleagues among adherent organisations and sister networks who supported the data collection process as well as focal points from development agencies, civil society organisations and local governments who took part in the survey at the country and global levels.

As this report was being prepared, an impressive number of new publications contributed to the collective thinking on implementing the nexus approach. Although too numerous to mention here, these have helped shape the drafting team thinking. Many of them can be found in the reference list.

The report was prepared by Dan Schreiber, Cushla Thompson, Júlia Codina Sariols and Kazuma Yabe. The team was co-ordinated by Dan Schreiber, with significant input from Sophia Swithern, under the strategic guidance of Cyprien Fabre and the general direction of Frederik Matthys. The team expresses particular thanks to Susan Sachs, the editor of the report, for her thoroughness, patience and availability.

The drafting team would also like to recognise the following people for their significant contributions at different stages of the review process: Kulani Abendroth-Dias, Peter Batchelor, Julie Belanger, Marie France Bourgeois, Angelica Broman, Paul Carr, Filiep Decorte, Tom Delrue, Martin Eklund, Réachbha FitzGerald, Mac Gordon Shaw, Orla Kelly, Sorie Lee, Mitch Levine, Betsy Lippman, Stephanie Loose, Hugh Macleman, Sajjad Malik, Keiko Matsuo, Jonathan Papoulidis, Martina Schmidt, Rachel Scott, Ryutaro Murotani, Christian Freres Kuer, Lydia Poole, Aaron Roesch, Carina Staibano and Marta Valdés. The team further recognises the many colleagues from DAC and UN adherent organisations and their partners based in DAC and partner countries for their support in implementing the global survey and other parts of the research for this report. The team would also like to thank colleagues from the World Bank, International Monetary Fund, Islamic Development Bank, Asian Development Bank and African Development Bank for their contributions as well as colleagues from VOICE, the Inter-Agency Standing Committee Results Group 4 and Reality of Aid for their interest and support.

Finally, the drafting team would like to thank Ola Kasneci, Sara Casadevall Bellés, Stephanie Coic and Henri-Bernard Solignac-Lecomte for their advice and support in preparing the document for publication.

Table of contents

FIGURES

INFOGRAPHICS

TABLES

Abbreviations and acronyms

ALNAP	Active Learning Network for Accountability and Performance in Humanitarian Action
CCA	Common country analysis
CSO	Civil society organisation
DAC	Development Assistance Committee (OECD)
DRR	Disaster risk reduction
EU	European Union
HC	Humanitarian Coordinator
HDP	Humanitarian, development and peace
IASC	Inter-Agency Standing Committee
IFI	International financial institution
IMF	International Monetary Fund
INCAF	International Network on Conflict and Fragility
INGO	International non-governmental organisation
IOM	International Organization for Migration
MDB	Multilateral development bank
NGO	Non-governmental organisation
ODA	Official development assistance
OECD	Organisation for Economic Co-operation and Development
PFM	Public financial management
RC	Resident Coordinator
RCO	Resident Coordinator's Office
SDC	Swiss Agency for Development and Cooperation
SDG	Sustainable Development Goal
Sida	Swedish International Development Cooperation Agency
UN	United Nations
UNDP	United Nations Development Programme
UNFPA	United Nations Population Fund

UN-Habitat	United Nations Human Settlements Programme
UNHCR	United Nations Refugee Agency
UNICEF	United Nations Children's Fund
WFP	World Food Programme

Executive summary

The Development Assistance Committee (DAC) Recommendation on the Humanitarian-Development-Peace Nexus is a unique, common standard aimed at enhancing the effectiveness of collective action in fragile and conflict-affected settings. In advance of the five-year review due by early 2024, this preliminary stocktaking exercise will facilitate joint learning, and feed the high-level Partnership for Peace roundtable in mid-2022.

Overall, one central message emerges: the strategic momentum around the DAC Recommendation must be seized to achieve its full potential.

Adherents to the DAC Recommendation have made visible efforts to implement it

- The DAC Recommendation is becoming a widely accepted common standard beyond its original signatories. With the adherence of UN entities, the policy dialogue about implementation is expanding to the multilateral system, allowing for a more consistent and meaningful execution of the nexus approach.

- Disseminating the DAC Recommendation's principles widely remains an important priority: they must translate into practical and concrete actions that inform organisational processes, partnerships and programming. Messages should be jargon-free and practice-oriented.

- The nexus approach has helped adherents to manage change within their organisations, each following different strategies, depending on timing, capacities, political will and individual trajectory.

- Adherents define success in implementing the nexus in various ways. From an operational standpoint, success may be defined both in terms of change in ways of working, and the achievement of sustainable outcomes improving lives in fragile contexts.

Progress has been made across the three areas of the DAC Recommendation

- Stakeholders have made significant progress in developing a shared understanding of how to reduce risks and improve resilience at country level, notably through the design of collective outcomes. However, co-ordination challenges remain, and joint analysis and joined-up planning must more meaningfully translate into programming.

- New operational practices reflecting the programming principles of the Recommendation are emerging. Identifying and scaling up good practices requires sustained collective investment in joint learning and evidence. There is little visible progress, however, in strengthening the voice and participation of people affected by crises and fragility.

- Similarly, the use of nexus-friendly financing models has increased somewhat over the past five years. It is important to learn from these initiatives and integrate them into the humanitarian and development financing architecture in a sustainable manner.

Table 1 summarises the status of implementation.

Important areas still need attention

- Short-term interventions for peace must, and can, be better connected to development objectives by enhancing mutual understanding and information sharing among HDP actors. Improving the "nexus literacy" of all these actors is fundamental in this regard.

- Achieving truly collective outcomes, with joined-up approaches to planning and programming agreed by all key stakeholders in a given context, would meaningfully advance coherence and complementarity.

- Inclusive financing strategies at country level could significantly accelerate nexus implementation, if designed to support major national processes, while fitting donor funding cycles as far as possible. Financing strategies are not the same as fundraising: they should include bilateral, multilateral and international financial institutions in a process that links financing and programming.

- Ensuring appropriate resourcing for cost-effective co-ordination remains a challenge. DAC adherents can do more to jointly support the existing co-ordination architecture and identify the best-fit leadership in every context.

- Political engagement and other tools, instruments and approaches remain underutilised in joined-up efforts across the nexus to prevent crises, resolve conflicts and build peace.

- The stakeholders closest to the affected communities should be included in a more meaningful way in joint planning processes, in particular local actors, civil society organisations, and national and international non-governmental organisations involved in implementing programmes.

- Investing in national and local capacities and systems cannot be an afterthought. Collective support and optimal use of public delivery systems for basic social services at national and local levels must remain a priority, even in times of crisis.

- The HDP nexus should integrate gender equality, climate change and other relevant considerations. It should not become a new, siloed policy area.

Table 1. A snapshot of the implementation of the DAC Recommendation

	PRINCIPLES OF THE DAC RECOMMENDATION	STATUS OF IMPLEMENTATION (See Chapter 2 for more details)
	CO-ORDINATION	
1.	Undertake **joint risk-informed, gender-sensitive analysis of root causes and structural drivers of conflict**, as well as positive factors of resilience and the identification of collective outcomes incorporating humanitarian, development and peace actions.	Meaningful progress, with widespread piloting of new approaches: adoption of collective outcomes in 24 out of 25 nexus pilot countries and contexts; experimentation with new tools and platforms for joint country analysis; and knowledge sharing and joint learning through the DAC-UN Dialogue. Bottlenecks: patchy evidence of meaningful commitment to deliver under one strategy; limited knowledge and application of guidance around the collective outcomes concept; actors' methodologies not always conducive to joined-up approaches. Further policy work is also needed on meaningful inclusion of local actors.
2.	Provide **appropriate resourcing to empower leadership** for cost-effective co-ordination across the humanitarian, development and peace architecture.	Leadership and co-ordination models vary greatly across contexts, with contrasting levels of perceived success. Overall, UN Resident Coordinators (RCs) and Humanitarian Coordinators (HCs) are seen as key providers of nexus leadership and co-ordination, ahead of national governments and key donors. Bottlenecks: ability, attention and capacity of national leadership; gap between expectations and resources for RC/HCs to support co-ordination across the nexus; and often limited donor co-ordination.
3.	Utilise **political engagement and other tools, instruments and approaches** at all levels to prevent crises, resolve conflicts and build peace.	Integration of the peace pillar remains at very early stage. A few initiatives have emerged to enhance how diplomatic, stabilisation and civilian security interventions join up and are coherent with humanitarian and development outcomes, but evidence is still anecdotal.
	PROGRAMMING	
4.	Prioritise **prevention, mediation and peacebuilding, investing in development whenever possible**, while ensuring immediate humanitarian needs continue to be met.	Preliminary evidence: while trends vary according to year and recipient country, overall there has been a gradual increase in the proportion of all donors' ODA to humanitarian needs and a gradual reduction in the share going towards development and peace, especially in extremely fragile contexts. Peace programming focuses more on basic

	PRINCIPLES OF THE DAC RECOMMENDATION	STATUS OF IMPLEMENTATION (See Chapter 2 for more details)
		safety and security in extremely fragile contexts than it does in other fragile contexts, where more ODA goes to core government functions. Inclusive political processes are a priority for donors across levels of fragility. In terms of policy, a few joint initiatives have emerged among DAC and IASC members and between UN adherents.
5.	Put **people at the centre**, tackling exclusion and promoting gender equality.	Both the humanitarian and development sectors have been striving to adopt more people-centred approaches for over a decade. No evidence was reviewed for this report of the extent to which the peace sector is implementing this principle. While it clearly links to the international women, peace and security agenda, there is scope to strengthen policy synergies and messaging about the contribution of gender sensitivity to the HDP nexus.
6.	Ensure that activities **do no harm**, are **conflict sensitive** to avoid unintended negative consequences and maximise positive effects across humanitarian, development and peace actions.	Use of conflict analysis to becoming more systematic among some of largest adherents. However, conflict and political economy analysis remain the least-used type of input for country analysis among survey respondents. More work is required to design suitable gender analysis methodologies that can be effectively integrated into programming. Policy research could help identify the determinants of successful collective outcomes in terms of social cohesion and conflict prevention.
7.	Align **joined-up programming with the risk environment.**	Evidence found in the humanitarian and development sectors of DAC and UN adherents of risk-informed programming that translates into change. COVID-19 and recent violent political transitions have put risk responsiveness to the test and led many adherents to start internal discussions on enhancing flexibility and anticipatory capacity.
8.	Strengthen **national and local capacities.**	Overall, national and subnational delivery is rarely the default option, despite positive examples. This principle is especially important for long-term development outcomes. Recent studies take stock of challenges in shifting a larger share of ODA to local organisations as well as advice on how to tackle these challenges. Linked to this principle, in 2021, the DAC adopted the Recommendation on Enabling Civil Society in Development Co-operation and Humanitarian Assistance.
9.	Invest in **learning and evidence** across humanitarian, development and peace actions.	An increasing number of actors engage in evaluating their performance in implementing the nexus approach, often focusing on either measures of impact or the degree to which their processes are fit for purpose. Questions remain on how to assess progress and ultimately ensure that the people affected by crises or fragility co-own such success . Further investment is also needed in developing evaluation approaches that span the nexus.
	FINANCING	
10.	Develop **evidence-based humanitarian, development and peace financing strategies** at global, regional, national and local levels, with effective layering and sequencing of the most appropriate financing flows.	Steps have been taken to develop financing strategy processes that bring together analysis and decisions on collective priorities, sources and funds, and strategic programming — for example in Democratic Republic of the Congo, Libya and Yemen. However, these remain standalone, unsystematised processes. The role of financing strategy processes in coalescing financing and prioritisation decisions has yet to be realised, and collective outcomes are still driven by multilateral actors rather than being truly inclusive. The majority of survey respondents reported that their team or organisation had never been involved in developing or aligning to financing strategies across the nexus.
11.	Use **predictable, flexible, multi-year financing** wherever possible.	The survey data, interviews and peer reviews make it clear that both the UN system and bilateral donors have made significant efforts to adjust their financing practices to support nexus approaches. In a growing number of examples, nexus-ready financing is enabling greater flexibility in response to contextual changes. In particular, progress has been made on financing instruments, approaches and individual projects, although these sometimes remain relatively siloed and nexus approaches have not yet been fully mainstreamed. But while some adherents have made organisational changes to provide more nexus-friendly financing, others face difficulties at organisational and/or parliamentary levels.

1 Seizing the Nexus Recommendation's full potential

The triple nexus approach rallies the broadest-ever coalition for change in fragile and conflict-affected settings. As such, implementing the DAC Recommendation on the Humanitarian-Development-Peace Nexus can help steer the "paradigm shift" or system-wide change called for at the World Humanitarian Summit in 2016. For this to happen, however, adherents must seize and sustain the strategic momentum that has been building around the DAC Recommendation.

This chapter first presents evidence of the momentum behind the nexus approach in general and the DAC Recommendation in particular. Next, it presents how adherents are translating the DAC Recommendation into their own institutions' policies and strategic approaches. It goes on to show that, while the DAC Recommendation is emerging as a widely accepted common standard, there is a continued need to disseminate its principles to a wider audience among DAC and UN Adherents and beyond, ensuring jargon-free and practice-oriented messaging. Finally, since implementing the DAC Recommendation is not an end in itself, the chapter explores the work that lies ahead at strategic level to better define what success looks like.

1.1. A widely accepted common standard

The Development Assistance Committee (DAC) Recommendation on the Humanitarian-Development-Peace Nexus (hereafter DAC Recommendation) aims to enhance the impact of international engagement in fragile and conflict-affected settings by providing its adherents a common set of principles to guide their approach. Experience from recent years with the nexus approach is already providing a substantive proof of concept that implementers of the DAC Recommendation can tap into and bring to scale. In addition, with the adherence of United Nations (UN) entities, the policy dialogue about implementation is expanding to the multilateral system, allowing for a more consistent and meaningful execution of the nexus approach. The DAC-UN Dialogue on implementing the DAC Recommendation has been an especially effective policy framework to start channelling the efforts of a growing, committed and active humanitarian, development and peace (HDP) community.

Visible change at country level

The DAC Recommendation builds on a change process that has been incrementally building up at country level over decades.[1] Global-level shifts beginning in the mid-2010s help explain the acceleration in recent years of country-level processes. Joined-up country planning processes across the HDP nexus, which began in 2015 in Haiti, are now taking place in 25 countries and contexts, according to mappings by the Inter-Agency Standing Committee (IASC) and the European Union (EU). Figure 1.1 illustrates the steady increase in the number of contexts where the nexus approach is being piloted, providing tangible evidence of the momentum for the nexus approach at field level.

Figure 1.1. Country-level implementation of the HDP nexus is increasing

Joined-up planning and programming have been initiated in new countries and contexts every year since 2015.

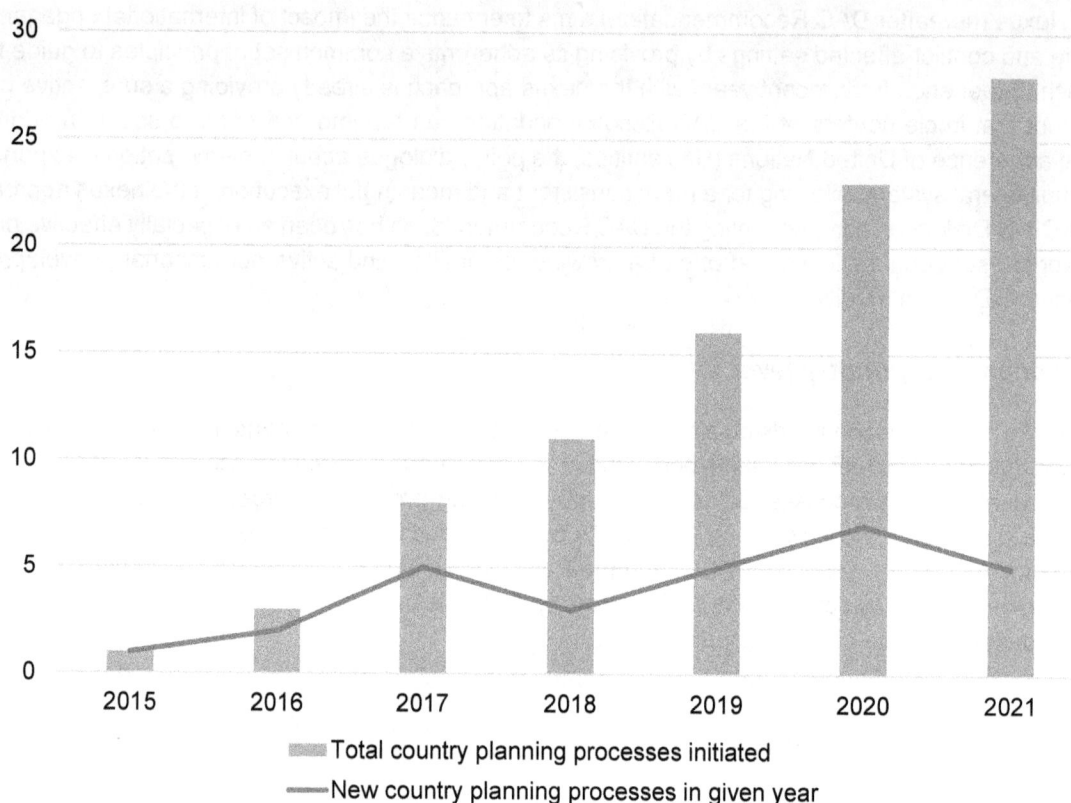

Total country planning processes initiated
New country planning processes in given year

Note: In general, the year that a country reports as the launch of its nexus pilot initiative is when a decisive step was taken in joined-up planning and programming processes that often were initiated earlier. The number of new country planning processes in any given year, indicated by the thin blue line, should be considered as indicative.
Source: For EU pilot projects, the EU Department for International Partnerships collected and provided information in the form of unpublished documents. For pilot contexts and countries initiated by UN RCs to operationalise the UN's new way of working: Inter-Agency Standing Committee (2021[1]), Mapping Good Practice in the Implementation of Peace Nexus Approaches: Synthesis Report, https://interagencystandingcommittee.org/system/files/2021-11/IASC%20Mapping%20of%20Good%20Practice%20in%20the%20Implementation%20of%20Humanitarian-Development%20Peace%20Nexus%20Approaches%2C%20Synthesis%20Report.pdf; UN (2018[2]), The New Way of Working – Country Progress Updates (webpage), https://www.un.org/jsc/content/new-way-working

This accelerating pace of country-level implementation is linked to two main global-level processes in particular. First, on the margins of the World Humanitarian Summit in 2016, the UN Secretary-General and executive heads of eight UN entities committed to implement a "new way of working" for humanitarian and development actors to carry forward the vision and "deliver better outcomes for people by moving beyond meeting their needs in the short term to reducing them over time" (UN, 2016[3]). This concept now guides the efforts of UN entities across the three pillars of the HDP nexus and of the World Bank Group at country level.[2] Advancing the new way of working involves establishing predictable and joint situation and problem analysis; better joined-up planning and programming; leadership and co-ordination by an empowered UN Resident Coordinator/Humanitarian Coordinator (RC/HC) with adequate capacity and resources; and financing modalities that can support collective outcomes (UN OCHA, 2017[4]). These different processes are also occurring in the context of the broader reform of the UN development system, whose ambition is to make it "fit for the purpose, opportunities and challenges presented by the 2030 Agenda", notably through a reinvigorated RC system and a new generation of country teams (UN, 2018[5]).

Second, a similar process has been taking place simultaneously within the EU. On 19 May 2017, as part of the EU's new strategic approach to resilience, the EU Council strengthened its commitment in a set of "conclusions" on operationalising the HDP nexus, encouraging the European Commission and EU member states to take forward joint analyses and, where possible, joint planning and programming of humanitarian and development partners (Council of the European Union, 2017[6]). A particular innovation in this regard was the explicit inclusion of a conflict prevention and peacebuilding component that requires humanitarian, development and peace actors to work together to address the root causes of fragility, vulnerability and conflict and to build resilience. In the 2017 European Consensus on Development, EU development partners also reinforced the principle of joint planning mentioned in the 2006 Consensus. This principle "puts joined-up EU and EU Member State actions at the heart of the implementation of development cooperation efforts" (Koenig and Brusset, 2019[7]).

Out of the 25 countries and contexts serving as pilot for the new way of working and/or the EU nexus pilots initiative (Infographic 1.1), 19 (or 76%) are categorised by the OECD as fragile contexts. Most of the pilot countries and contexts (13) are in sub-Saharan Africa; six are in the Middle East and North Africa region, four are in Eastern Europe and Asia, and two are in South America and the Caribbean. Stakeholders across the nexus are focusing joint planning and joined-up programming efforts on a range of thematic areas to varying degrees. The most common of these is peace and human security (e.g. promoting social cohesion, enhancing people's safety and security, and addressing gender-based violence), with 16 pilot contexts featuring efforts in this area. Joint efforts also focus on food security and economic resilience in 15 of the pilot contexts; on access to basic social services in 14; on forced displacement in 13; on efforts to strengthen the coping capacity of local systems and the resilience of communities in the face of climate change in nine; and/or on other factors of risk in seven of the pilot contexts.

Country-level processes have largely developed organically, building on existing mechanisms and planning processes. This also means that the success of such processes so far remains highly dependent on a combination of sustained and committed leadership from RC/HC and/or European leadership and co-ordination; key partners' willingness to commit; and in many cases, the roll-out of a robust humanitarian co-ordination architecture. There remains much untapped opportunity cross-fertilisation across contexts.

Infographic 1.1. Nexus pilot countries: an overview

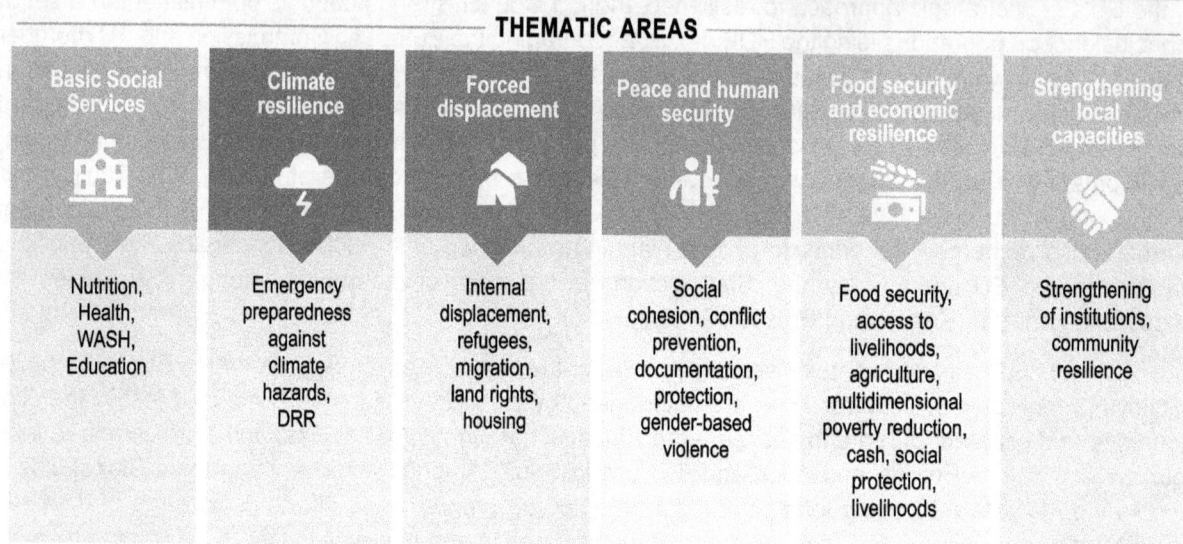

THEMATIC AREAS

Basic Social Services	Climate resilience	Forced displacement	Peace and human security	Food security and economic resilience	Strengthening local capacities
Nutrition, Health, WASH, Education	Emergency preparedness against climate hazards, DRR	Internal displacement, refugees, migration, land rights, housing	Social cohesion, conflict prevention, documentation, protection, gender-based violence	Food security, access to livelihoods, agriculture, multidimensional poverty reduction, cash, social protection, livelihoods	Strengthening of institutions, community resilience

Sub-Saharan Africa

COUNTRY	FRAMEWORK	YEAR STARTED	Basic Social Services	Climate resilience	Forced displacement	Peace and human security	Food security and economic resilience	Strengthening local capacities
BURKINA FASO	NWOW, EU	2017	●	●		●	●	
BURUNDI	NWOW	2021		●			●	●
CAMEROON	NWOW	2019	●			●	●	
CENTRAL AFRICAN REPUBLIC	NWOW, EU	2020				●	●	●
CHAD	NWOW, EU	UN 2017, EU 2020	●				●	
DEMOCRATIC REPUBLIC OF THE CONGO	NWOW	2019	●		●	●	●	
ETHIOPIA	NWOW	2018			●			
MAURITANIA	NWOW	2018	●	●		●	●	
MOZAMBIQUE	EU	-	●	●		●		
NIGERIA	NWOW	EU 2017, UN 2018	●		●	●	●	
SOMALIA	NWOW	2020	●	●	●	●	●	●
SUDAN	NWOW, EU	2019	●		●	●		
UGANDA	EU	2018	●	●	●	●		

EU: European Union pilot initiative | NWOW: New Way of Working

South America and the Caribbean

COUNTRY	FRAMEWORK	YEAR STARTED	THEMATIC AREAS OF THE PILOT
COLOMBIA	NWOW	2020	
HAITI	NWOW, EU	EU 2015, UN 2021	

Middle East and North Africa

COUNTRY	FRAMEWORK	YEAR STARTED	THEMATIC AREAS OF THE PILOT
IRAQ	NWOW, EU	2021	
JORDAN	NWOW	2016	
LEBANON	NWOW, EU	2017	
LIBYA	NWOW	2019	
WEST BANK AND GAZA STRIP*	NWOW	2020	
YEMEN	NWOW, EU	2016	

Eastern Europe and Asia

COUNTRY	FRAMEWORK	YEAR STARTED	THEMATIC AREAS OF THE PILOT
AFGHANISTAN	NWOW, EU	2020	
MYANMAR	NWOW, EU	2020	
PHILIPPINES	EU	-	
UKRAINE	NWOW	2017	

EU: European Union pilot initiative | NWOW: New Way of Working

THEMATIC AREAS: Basic Social Services, Climate resilience, Forced displacement, Peace and human security, Food security and economic resilience, Strengthening local capacities

Thematic areas under development

Note: The thematic areas in the infographic represent a synthesis of key objectives defined through joined-up processes involving actors across the nexus, mainly in the form of collective outcomes. The table indicates whether these are processes conducted in pilot countries of the New Way of Working, the EU Nexus pilot initiative, or both.
Source: See Figure 1.1 for all the list of sources.

A growing, committed and active triple nexus community

The adherence of seven UN entities (and counting) is a sign that the DAC Recommendation is having an impact beyond its original signatories. It has emerged as a widely accepted, shared global standard to foster change in how organisations act and interact, including by building a growing HDP community that shares a commitment to and common principles for improving lives and outcomes. Box 1.1 describes the nexus approach and aims of each of the seven UN adherents.

Beyond strategic commitment, the expanding collaboration between DAC and UN adherents is already delivering early results. The DAC-UN Dialogue on the implementation of the DAC Recommendation, launched by the International Network on Conflict and Fragility (INCAF) in line with the outcome document of the Partnership for Peace high-level Roundtable in October 2020, serves as a problem-solving platform. Co-led by the United States and the World Food Programme (WFP), the DAC-UN Dialogue more broadly aims to foster joined-up implementation of the DAC Recommendation in fragile and conflict-affected contexts. Its work has been driven through two work streams:

- The trilingualism work stream, co-led by the Japan International Cooperation Agency and the the United Nations Development Programme (UNDP), aims to "ensure that the right people are deployed in the right place and at the right time and are doing the right things to support more joined-up complementary nexus approaches to tackling the drivers of fragility", according to the (unpublished) January 2022 "offer document" of the DAC-UN Dialogue. This entails supporting a step change in the capacity of staff at all levels to understand how to engage with stakeholders from the humanitarian, development and peace pillars, as well as ensuring enhanced understanding of opportunities to strengthen coherence and complementarity. The first objective of this work stream was to produce an integrated nexus training package, knowledge platform and ongoing support facility through the establishment of the Nexus Academy. The official launch of the academy was in February 2022.

- The co-ordination in countries work stream, co-led by Belgium and the International Organization for Migration (IOM), aims to provide a shared space where stakeholders involved in the HDP nexus can exchange on instruments for joint context analysis and joined-up programming in line with the DAC Recommendation. It also provides country support upon request. To date, it has identified Mozambique and Niger as pilot countries and has engaged UN RCOs. This workstream also has launched a series of webinars focused on processes and tools to improve in-country planning and co-ordination.

Box 1.1. The United Nations adherents to the DAC Recommendation and the HDP nexus

Between October 2019 and November 2021, seven UN entities submitted applications and were accepted by the OECD as new adherents to the DAC Recommendation. In addition, in February 2021, the UN Deputy Secretary-General announced that the UN Secretariat fully subscribes to the Recommendation. These developments have further strengthened the strategic momentum around it and enhanced its significance.

United Nations Development Programme (UNDP)

The Nexus Academy, delivered as a common good on behalf of the DAC-UN Dialogue and hosted by the UNDP, facilitates joint learning and knowledge exchange to accelerate nexus approaches. The UNDP also provides global leadership on nexus approaches through its roles in the UN Joint Steering Committee to Advance Humanitarian and Development Collaboration, the IASC Results Group on the nexus, and the trilingualism work stream of the DAC-UN Dialogue. At regional and country level, the UNDP has been promoting operationalisation of the HDP nexus through tailored support and is developing differentiated approaches in Afghanistan, Myanmar and elsewhere to ensure that development approaches that complement ongoing and vital humanitarian response are maintained.

United Nations Human Settlement Programme (UN-Habitat)

UN-Habitat fosters integrated approaches for urban areas in the HDP nexus to address root causes and drivers of conflict such as land and spatial inequality; promote sustainable urban development and area-based approaches; support urban recovery and inclusive multi-level governance; and facilitate social inclusion in cities. To align further with the HDP nexus, it is strengthening the UN system-wide approach to sustainable urban development and supporting urban profiling that ensures participatory, locally-owned and tailored governance processes. The agency has also provided assistance to local governments and cities to engage in UN-supported processes, including the elaboration of Common Country Analyses and Cooperation Frameworks[3] and managing displacement.

World Food Programme (WFP)

On the co-ordination side, the WFP is committing to joint analysis and programming at country level, including collective outcomes that reduce humanitarian needs; strengthened co-ordination between agencies and within the WFP alongside global and headquarters-level policy development that promotes HDP approaches; advocacy for the centrality of food security for longer-term, sustainable peace and development outcomes; and capacity strengthening on nexus approaches, among other actions. Initiatives in programming include ensuring full investment in relevant work plans, particularly those related to conflict sensitivity, as well as a focus on the role of the nexus in famine prevention and redesigning of programmes.

United Nations Children's Fund (UNICEF)

UNICEF's *Strategic Plan 2022-2025* and revised Core Commitments to Children in Humanitarian Action include key commitments and considerations on linking humanitarian, development, conflict sensitivity, and contributions to peacebuilding and social cohesion. The recently conducted *Formative Evaluation of UNICEF Work to Link Humanitarian and Development Programming* provides insights and recommendations for practical improvements in UNICEF's approach to strengthen the coherence and complementarity of programmes within its dual mandate.

International Organization for Migration (IOM)

The IOM has been conducting an evaluation of different countries' implementation of the nexus to identify best practices. The IOM is also mainstreaming the nexus approach through advisors, staff training and internal capacity development. The HDP nexus is also part of a broader framework that will be submitted for approval and has been shared with regional offices to ensure it becomes part of the UN Common Country Analyses. The IOM Migration Crisis Operational Framework already promotes stronger linkages between its sectors of assistance in the humanitarian, peace and security, and development areas.

United Nations Population Fund (UNFPA)

UNFPA programming engages partners at individual, community and national levels including by strengthening the capacities of local women and youth groups and government authorities to enhance basic services and address inequalities. The HDP nexus has been streamlined into its programming, and operational and structural shifts have taken place to further align with the nexus.

United Nations High Commissioner for Refugees (UNHCR)

UNHCR is building stronger synergies with HDP actors to prevent or mitigate conflict and protracted displacement; work towards common objectives, such as the Sustainable Development Goals (SDGs); and ensure the inclusion of refugees, IDPs, stateless persons, and returnees into development planning and programming. It has considerably increased its engagement with multilateral development banks and bilateral development actors on the HDP nexus, including to develop a shared understanding of the root causes of crises and protracted forced displacement. The Global Compact on Refugees and the Global Refugee Forum in 2023 offer an opportunity to assess progress and chart the way forward towards implementation of the HDP Recommendation in protracted displacement situations.

Source: Interviews and written consultation with UN adherents.

1.2. The triple nexus as change management

Much can be learned from the way adherents are already taking forward the nexus approach. While many adherent organisations have started integrating the triple nexus approach into their strategic and policy frameworks, they also need to ensure that their institutional systems and processes are adapted to implementation of this approach. The DAC Recommendation can serve as a compass for such institutional change. A review of internal processes finds three broad institutional approaches in use: grand strategies, bottom-up approaches and targeted measures. For each adherent, timing, capacities, political will and an assessment of its individual trajectory will dictate which change strategy is most appropriate. Some of the necessary changes require a profound shift in institutional mind-set. In particular, there is an opportunity to reframe integrity and risk and think about how the nexus can increase accountability to taxpayers.

Updating organisational policies to integrate the nexus approach

It is a fundamental principle of international norms that every adherent must ensure that its own policies and practices are consistent with the norms. In consequence, DAC and UN adherents have been progressively revising their strategic plans and policies to ensure consistency with the DAC Recommendation. For example, Austria, Belgium, the Czech Republic, Denmark, the EU, Germany, Ireland, Japan, Korea, Norway, Portugal, Sweden, the United Kingdom and the United States have all explicitly outlined specific positions and ways of working to enhance the coherence of their efforts across the HDP nexus. Most DAC adherents have reported new or ongoing ways in which they are incorporating the HDP approach into their internal processes and policies. For example, Denmark has had a joint strategy for co-ordinating humanitarian and development assistance since 2017, which was further revised in 2021. Sweden's 2016 policy framework and the United Kingdom's 2015 aid strategy, both of which predate the adoption of the DAC Recommendation, are additional examples of close alignment with the principles of the DAC Recommendation.[4]

Adherents are managing nexus-friendly change in various ways

Across bilateral providers of official development assistance, humanitarian and development programming is often managed by separate siloed entities or different ministries and agencies. Bilateral co-operation agencies tend to have programmatic and budgetary control over humanitarian and/or development activities but limited influence on diplomatic and security engagement in fragile and conflict-affected settings. Relatedly, DAC members' efforts to improve whole-of-government co-ordination in fragile and conflict-affected contexts do not necessarily translate into greater programme coherence across the HDP nexus.[5]

Nevertheless, there is evidence that many adherents have started making the necessary operational changes to implement the triple nexus approach. The different types of initiatives undertaken at headquarters level to promote change reflect each organisation's institutional opportunities and constraints, which are especially dictated by support from the political leadership, the capacity of current institutions to absorb the change or intervention, and the existence of a policy window (OECD, 2019[8]). Adherents' strategies to promote change and move forward towards the nexus can be grouped into three broad types of activity:

- **Grand strategy approaches** involve extensive legislative redesign efforts or other types of strategic initiatives aimed at rethinking organisational processes and rewiring institutional frameworks. While they requires a unique combination of circumstances, several major bilateral and multilateral actors have nonetheless adopted this type of approach. Notable examples of such strategic initiatives include the United States' Global Fragility Act of 2019 (Hume et al., 2020[9]; Yayboke et al., 2021[10]); the World Bank Group's *Fragility, Conflict and Violence Strategy 2020-2025* (World Bank Group, 2019[11]); the Global Compact for Refugees of 2018, with the UNHCR acting as institutional sponsor; and Belgium's 2018 general policy note on international development (OECD, 2020[12]).

  Example: The Global Fragility Act, enacted by the United States in 2019, requires joined-up humanitarian, prevention and development programmes to promote conflict prevention and stability when relevant. It sets out commitments to improve the global, regional and local co-ordination of relevant international and multilateral development and donor organisations; to include specific objectives and multi-sectoral approaches to reduce fragility; and to adopt approaches that ensure national leadership where appropriate as well as participatory engagement by local and national actors.

- **Bottom-up approaches** drive incremental reform by cultivating internal coalitions for change, promote iterative joint learning and gradually integrate new approaches into the broader organisation. This type of approach is a deliberative process entailing sustained effort and the search for opportunities and internal champions. Unlike the grand strategy approach, a bottom-up approach does not necessarily require early commitment from the strategic top of the organisation; rather, middle management or policy functions may initially facilitate and foster their emergence. Examples of this approach include Switzerland's nexus learning journey (Box 1.3); the Global Affairs Canada internal nexus working group; UN-Habitat's new collective results framework that promoted a shift of mind-sets; and practical action at programme level by Sweden and the United Kingdom (FAO, Development Initiatives and Norwegian Refugee Council, 2021[13]).

Example: Switzerland's nexus learning journey was designed as an iterative process to move from a double to a triple nexus understanding through learning from good practices and analysing bottlenecks. Focus discussions among headquarters staff and field interviews helped Switzerland generate the broad buy-in and ownership that are crucial for nexus operationalisation. The thinking process has been mainstreamed, and concrete proposals for change as well as the continued deployment of nexus advisors are being discussed.

- **Targeted measures** give strategic impetus to the nexus approach in critical areas such as staffing and training, funding mechanisms, co-ordination structures, operational tools, and new relevant partnerships. This approach is more circumscribed but allows for effective action and can be intra-organisational and/or inter-organisational.

    Examples: There are multiple noteworthy examples of the target measures approach including Germany's new transitional development assistance instrument; Sweden's deployment of nexus advisors; the multidimensional context analysis tools developed by various bilateral and multilateral donors; the Nexus Academy, a common good developed within the DAC-UN Dialogue with support from the UNDP; the UNICEF Guidance for Risk-Informed Programming; Korea's design of a new HDP nexus strategy; the commissioning of external evaluations of nexus-related effectiveness by several UN adherents, among them the IOM and UNICEF; and the inclusion of nexus-related monitoring indicators as part of the new generation of strategic plans by various UN adherents.

Some of these critical changes require profound adjustments in not only rules, but also institutional mind-sets, as existing flexibilities are not always used. There may be an opportunity in terms of how integrity, risk and effectiveness are framed as part of accountability to taxpayers. One revealing comment from interviews was that "sometimes it seems that more energy is spent chasing the USD 2 not accounted for, than ensuring the USD 2 million is spent on the right thing".

1.3. Bridging the gap between support and implementation

There is broad acceptance of the value of the nexus approach. Despite this, disseminating the DAC Recommendation's principles widely remains an important priority to translate it into concrete actions that inform organisational processes, partnerships and programming. It is important to keep the messages jargon-free and practice-oriented.

Broad acceptance of the value of the nexus approach

The Nexus Interim Report Survey, undertaken for this report, found that a commanding majority of respondents — 98% — agree or strongly agree that a coherent approach to humanitarian, development and peace activities offers more potential benefits than risks or drawbacks.

Figure 1.2. Perceptions of the nexus approach's risk-to-benefit ratio

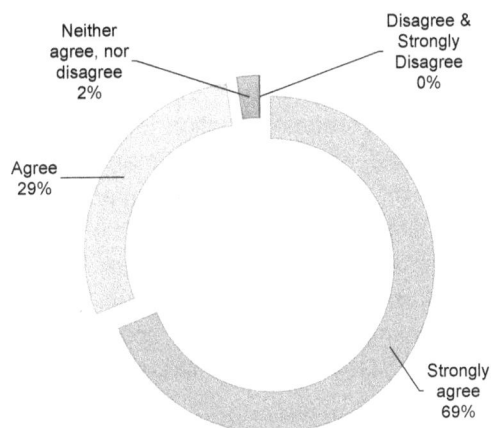

Note: The figure shows the degree to which survey respondents agreed with the following statement: "Overall, I believe that a coherent approach between humanitarian, development and peace activities carries more potential benefits than potential risks or downsides."
Source: Nexus Interim Report Survey

Moreover, 44% of all respondents said they see a change in coherence and complementarity following the adoption of the nexus approach – and this score reaches 70% among respondents most likely to be involved in nexus planning and co-ordination activities (such as those in roles supporting RC/HCs).

Figure 1.3. Perceptions of contributions of the HDP nexus approach to a coherent and complementary collective response

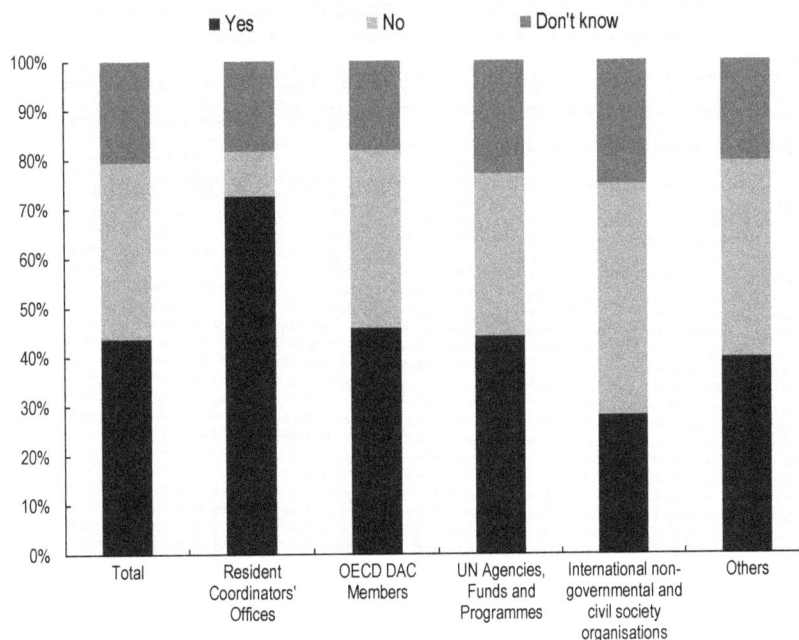

Note: The figure shows survey responses, by type of organisation, to the question: "Have you seen any change in the coherence and complementarity of the collective response as a result of adopting a nexus approach in your geographic area of responsibility?" Answers are broken down by respondents according to where they work – in a UN RC office (RCO); a DAC member; a UN agency, fund or programme (AFP); an international non-governmental organisation (INGO) or civil society organisation (CSO); and others
Source: Nexus Interim Report Survey

Disseminating the DAC Recommendation's principles remains a priority

While there is broad acceptance of the nexus approach, a review of policy literature and consultations with INCAF members show a continuing need to disseminate the DAC Recommendation's principles to a wider audience, both among adherents and beyond. One of the most frequently heard comment from those consulted for this report is that the DAC Recommendation did not come with an instruction manual for proper implementation – although some adherents have started to fill that gap (Box 1.4). A related challenge, discussed in section 3.1, is to reassure humanitarian actors that in politically charged contexts, co-ordination across the triple nexus takes into account the need to preserve humanitarian space. In other situations, applying the HDP nexus approach can also seem daunting, as it demands a thorough reassessment of current practice. How, then, can humanitarian, development and peace actors judge whether they are effectively implementing the triple nexus approach? This concern appears to be very much alive among DAC adherents to the Nexus Recommendation.

Moreover, adherents to the DAC Recommendation represent a diverse set of institutions ranging from bilateral and multilateral organisations to ministries, executive agencies and bilateral development banks, each with its own organisational culture and areas of expertise. As a result, the extent to which one organisation's practical guidance for implementing the DAC Recommendation aligns with the policies of others is of understandable concern to adherents. The good news is that the survey and literature review conducted for this report found little evidence that organisational differences among adherents are resulting in conflicting interpretations of the HDP nexus approach. This common ground reflects the fact that many of the concepts set forth in the DAC Recommendation have emerged over the course of many years, if not decades.

Nevertheless, a fundamental question remains to be answered: How can actors know that their adopted approach is, in fact, applying the triple nexus? In this regard, the development of jargon-free and practice-oriented messages can help practitioners at country level focus, first on the core elements that matter most for the collective implementation of the nexus approach. Interviews with nexus specialists from some DAC members suggest that such distilled messaging on the core features of the triple nexus approach are already common practice in some organisations and can provide effective support to country-level activities. Box 1.2 compiles the core features cited by respondents in these interviews. A review of recent guidance developed to help field practitioners apply the triple nexus approach confirms that these elements are widely perceived as critical (Swedish International Development Cooperation Agency, 2020[14]; CARE Canada, 2019[15]; Hövelmann, 2020[16]; Zamore, 2019[17]; FAO, Development Initiatives and Norwegian Refugee Council, 2021[13]).

Box 1.2. How do you know you are effectively "nexus-ing"?

A triple nexus approach that contributes to more effective interventions in fragile and conflict-affected contexts should aim to incorporate all of the following core features:

- a long-term focus on reducing overall vulnerability and unmet needs and addressing root causes of crises
- sustained efforts to foster inclusive country leadership and support local capacities
- a priority focus on those most at risk or left behind, with support for equal fulfilment of basic needs for all and gender equality
- consideration and active management of risks including conflict sensitivity and do no harm
- an approach, operational set-up and/or financing mechanisms that help navigate short-term realities and the evolving context without losing sight of long-term development perspectives
- awareness of the interventions of other humanitarian, peace and development actors and joint efforts to prioritise, focus on comparative advantages and enhance coherence.

Note: The 11 principles of the DAC Recommendation are an indivisible whole. This presentation of what are identified as core elements is not a redefinition of the agreed HDP nexus framework, but rather the starting point for a journey that involves all facets of the DAC Recommendation.

Source: Interviews and written consultation with adherents.

1.4. The challenge of defining success

The triple nexus approach is a means, not an end. It needs to be founded on a clear vision of what collective success looks like that can be evaluated and evolve based on joint learning. Indeed, how success is defined can evolve over the course of the nexus learning journey. It is thus important to carve out space for this discussion to happen among adherents at both policy and high-level decision-making level.

Box 1.3. Building a coalition for change: Switzerland's learning journey approach

Switzerland provides a useful example of a deliberately bottom-up approach to nexus-minded organisational change and demonstrates how the definition of success in implementing the nexus approach evolves over time. The process started in 2018 when the Swiss Agency for Development and Cooperation (SDC) commissioned an independent evaluation of its implementation of the double (humanitarian-development) nexus. The evaluation covered staff from all SDC departments at the agency's head office and the field and included field visits and data collection from various contexts. The evaluation, published in 2019, concluded that the SDC is viewed as "a principled donor with a strong focus on context" and advised the agency "to enhance a conducive institutional set-up at head office in order to institutionalise the nexus approach and make it less person- and opportunity-driven".

The SDC's management endorsed the recommendations, prompting the agency to embark on what it termed a learning journey. This process was designed to learn from good practices and analyse bottlenecks with the aim of fostering organisational learning about how to implement the nexus approach. Gradually, the process incorporated questions around how to better integrate the peace pillar of the nexus into the SDC approach. A core group that consults regularly with a broader set of nexus constituents carries the process forward. The main steps of the process include a review of state-of-the-art examples from the field that Switzerland is contributing to as well as numerous interviews of field and headquarters staff and non-governmental organisation partners. Various intermediary steps were built into the process to disseminate learning and build buy-in across the organisation.

Concurrently with the initial phase of the learning journey, SDC management decided to reorganise the agency and integrate the nexus approach into its change strategy. As a demonstration of strong political support for the nexus approach, this served as an additional catalyst for change. The active participation of headquarters and field staff has helped increase acceptance and ownership of the process within the organisation. The SDC is also preparing in-depth sessions on specific thematic areas that need attention such as climate change, forced displacement and education, peace and governance, and equality. The conclusions of these sessions will be published in a report that will also present ideas on how to move forward, building on the strong collective momentum.

Source: Nordic Consulting Group Denmark (2019[18]) *Independent Evaluation of the Linkage of Humanitarian Aid and Development Cooperation at the Swiss Development Cooperation*, https://www.alnap.org/help-library/independent-evaluation-of-the-linkage-of-humanitarian-aid-and-development-cooperation; 2021 interview with SDC staff.

Success must be defined in operational, as well as in strategic terms

The implementation of the DAC Recommendation as a framework for progress will require the development of pragmatic, realistic and measurable objectives for reducing humanitarian needs, risk and vulnerability in relevant contexts. From this standpoint, adherents define success in implementing the nexus in two complementary ways, namely in terms of changes in the way of working and in the achievement of sustainable outcomes improving lives in fragile contexts. This two-pronged approach is also seen in the different ways adherents are starting to monitor progress against the nexus approach, discussed in Chapter 2.

A focus on shifting the way of working and on achieving outcomes that benefit people offers a useful set of benchmarks. However, defining what success looks like involves broader collective, strategic questions. Indeed, DAC adherents have found that while some of their structures and policies need to be adjusted, it is often culture and political economy rather than hard barriers that need to be addressed. These include achieving enhanced inclusion of the peace dimension and peace actors; greater attention to building coherence and complementarity between (rather than just within) institutions; and creating the right institutional mind-sets and incentives.

A pragmatic approach is needed

Case studies show that field actors in various contexts tend to set unrealistic collective outcomes, establish unfeasible indicators of success or turn a blind eye to unavoidable obstacles (Veron and Hauck, 2021[19]; Zürcher, 2020[20]). This suggests that stakeholders need to infuse joined-up planning and programming with realism, focus and humility (Brown, 2020[21]). A more pragmatic approach is also needed when developing guidance for the implementation of the nexus approach. There is a tendency to formulate guidance on the nexus approach that is too abstract and not sufficiently connected to everyday working realities in fragile contexts (Südhoff, Hövelmann and Steinke, 2020[22]). In the absence of applicable approaches, however, there is a risk that nexus implementation will simply involve changing the labels of activities already in current practice.

Box 1.4. Organisational guidance on operationalising the nexus: The example of Sweden

Among available guidance documents to help field practitioners apply the triple nexus approach, that of the Swedish International Development Cooperation Agency (Sida), stands out as a particularly useful available example for other adherents, by aligning closely with the logic and scope of the DAC Recommendation.

Sida issued its guidance note after the DAC Recommendation was adopted and following the 2019 OECD Development Co-operation Peer Review of Sweden, which identified a need for a more systematic approach to linking humanitarian with development work. The guidance note aims to provide concrete guidance to Sida staff and guide the agency's dialogue with partners and other donors. It builds on Sida's analysis of its own good practices in co-ordination, analysis and financing at country level and reviews what Sida should do across the three dimensions of the nexus to operationalise the DAC Recommendation's principles. For example, the Sida guidance note points out opportunities for engagement with multilateral partners on the HDP nexus such as the EU, UN and World Bank nexus pilot approaches.

More recently, comparable efforts have started to develop among other DAC adherents, including Canada, Italy and the United States.

Source: Swedish International Development Cooperation Agency (2020[14]), *Guidance Note for Sida: Humanitarian-Development-Peace Nexus*, https://cdn.sida.se/publications/files/sida62325en-humanitarian-development--peace-nexus.pdf.

The HDP nexus approach has largely developed organically, and the DAC Recommendation provides an opportunity to set clear and measurable system-wide expectations. At both country and global level, the most successful models have been largely driven by self-selecting coalitions of willing individuals and institutions identifying specific, practical opportunities. This is the obvious and best way to start, as it provides opportunities to test out approaches before moving to scale. It is now time for a wider set of actors and resources to engage, particularly beyond the UN system. Ultimately, any definition of success must be (co-)owned by the people affected by crises or fragility or their legitimate representatives.

References

Brown, S. (2020), "The Rise and Fall of the Aid Effectiveness Norm", *European Journal of Development Research*, Vol. 32/4, pp. 1230-1248, https://doi.org/10.1057/s41287-020-00272-1.
[21]

CARE Canada (2019), *Annual Impact and Learning Review: The Humanitarian-Development Nexus*, https://reliefweb.int/sites/reliefweb.int/files/resources/Nexus_FINAL_EXTERNAL_200415.pdf (accessed on 22 June 2021).
[15]

Council of the European Union (2017), *Conclusions on Operationalising the Humanitarian-Development Nexus*, https://www.consilium.europa.eu/media/24010/nexus-st09383en17.pdf.
[6]

FAO, Development Initiatives and Norwegian Refugee Council (2021), *Development Actors at the Nexus: Lessons from Crises in Bangladesh, Cameroon and Somalia - Synthesis Report*, Food and Agricultural Organization, Rome, https://doi.org/10.4060/cb3835en.
[13]

Hövelmann, S. (2020), *Triple Nexus to Go*, Centre for Humanitarian Action, Berlin, https://www.chaberlin.org/wp-content/uploads/2020/03/2020-03-triple-nexus-to-go-hoevelmann-en-online.pdf (accessed on 22 June 2021).
[16]

Hume, E. et al. (2020), *Getting From Here to There: Successful Implementation of the Global Fragility Act*, Alliance for Peacebuilding, Washington, DC, https://allianceforpeacebuilding.app.box.com/s/5t5gs6ihc9lubw29sr2btjciy3cdeudf.
[9]

Inter-Agency Standing Committee (2021), *Mapping Good Practice in the Implementation of Peace Nexus Approaches: Synthesis Report*, https://interagencystandingcommittee.org/system/files/2021-11/IASC%20Mapping%20of%20Good%20Practice%20in%20the%20Implementation%20of%20Humanitarian-Development%20Peace%20Nexus%20Approaches%2C%20Synthesis%20Report.pdf.
[1]

Koenig, S. and E. Brusset (2019), *Joint Programming in Conflict-Affected and Fragile States*, European Commission, Brussels.
[7]

Nordic Consulting Group Denmark (2019), *Independent Evaluation of the Linkage of Humanitarian Aid and Development Cooperation at the Swiss Development Cooperation*, Swiss Agency for Development and Cooperation, Bern, https://www.alnap.org/help-library/independent-evaluation-of-the-linkage-of-humanitarian-aid-and-development-cooperation.
[18]

OECD (2020), *States of Fragility 2020*, OECD Publishing, Paris, https://doi.org/10.1787/ba7c22e7-en.
[12]

OECD (2019), *DAC Recommendation on the Humanitarian-Development-Peace Nexus*, OECD/LEGAL/5019, OECD Publishing, Paris, https://legalinstruments.oecd.org/en/instruments/OECD-LEGAL-5019.
[8]

Südhoff, R., S. Hövelmann and A. Steinke (2020), *The Triple Nexus in Practice: Challenges and Options for Multi-Mandated Organisations*, Centre for Humanitarian Action, Berlin, https://www.chaberlin.org/wp-content/uploads/dlm_uploads/2021/06/2020-11-12-chavocado-update-21-for-web.pdf (accessed on 18 January 2022).
[22]

Swedish International Development Cooperation Agency (2020), *Guidance Note for Sida: Humanitarian-Development-Peace Nexus*, https://cdn.sida.se/publications/files/sida62325en-humanitarian-development--peace-nexus.pdf. [14]

UN (2018), *The New Way of Working - Country Progress Updates (webpage)*, https://www.un.org/jsc/content/new-way-working. [2]

UN (2018), *UN Development System Reform 101 (webpage)*, https://reform.un.org/content/un-development-system-reform-101 (accessed on 12 February 2022). [5]

UN (2016), *Transcending Humanitarian-Development Divides: Changing People's Lives from Delivering Aid to Ending*, https://agendaforhumanity.org/sites/default/files/WHS Commitment to action - transcending humanitarian-development divides_0.pdf. [3]

UN OCHA (2017), *New Way of Working*, United Nations Office for the Coordination of Humanitarian Affairs (OCHA), New York, https://www.unocha.org/sites/unocha/files/NWOW%20Booklet%20low%20res.002_0.pdf (accessed on 29 June 2020). [4]

Veron, P. and V. Hauck (2021), "Connecting the pieces of the puzzle: The EU's implementation of the humanitarian-development-peace nexus", *Discussion Paper*, No. 301, European Centre for Development Policy Management, Maastricht, Netherlands, https://ecdpm.org/wp-content/uploads/Connecting-Pieces-Puzzle-EU-Implementation-Humanitarian-Development-Peace-Nexus-ECDPM-Discussion-Paper-301-2021.pdf (accessed on 25 June 2021). [19]

World Bank Group (2019), *Strategy for Fragility, Conflict, and Violence 2020-2025*, https://documents1.worldbank.org/curated/en/844591582815510521/pdf/World-Bank-Group-Strategy-for-Fragility-Conflict-and-Violence-2020-2025.pdf. [11]

Yayboke, E. et al. (2021), *A Policymaker's Guide to the Global Fragility Act*, Center for Strategic and International Studies, Washington, DC, https://www.csis.org/analysis/policymakers-guide-global-fragility-act. [10]

Zamore, L. (2019), *The Triple Nexus in Practice: Toward a New Way of Working in Protracted and Repeated Crises*, Center on International Cooperation, New York, https://cic.nyu.edu/sites/default/files/triple-nexus-in-practice-nwow-full-december-2019-web.pdf (accessed on 29 June 2020). [17]

Zürcher, C. (2020), *Meta-Review of Evaluations of Development Assistance to Afghanistan, 2008-2018 - Chapeau Paper*, Federal Ministry for Economic Cooperation and Development, Bonn, https://www.sicherheitneudenken.de/media/download/variant/198198 (accessed on 22 September 2021). [20]

Notes

[1] For a comprehensive overview of the lineage of the triple nexus approach from different perspectives, see, among other source materials, https://www.alnap.org/help-library/ngo-perspectives-on-the-eus-humanitarian-development-peace-nexus; https://www.dropbox.com/s/smy3t02ovt5y6mm/SGDE-EDRMS-%239939660-v1-Triple%20nexus%20in%20the%20DRC_final_EN.pdf?dl=0; and https://csopartnership.org/resource/localizing-the-triple-nexus-policy-research-on-humanitarian-developement-and-peace-nexus-in-9-contexts/?wpdmdl=17681&refresh=61c273ffbd36d1640133631.

[2] The UN has also established the Joint Steering Committee to guide policy setting and foster synergies in humanitarian and development action to achieve progress on the Sustainable Development Goals. See https://www.un.org/jsc/sites/www.un.org.jsc/files/general/tors_of_the_jsc.pdf. Additionally, under the banner of the Humanitarian-Development-Peace Initiative, the UN and World Bank Group have jointly committed to "identify collective outcomes and deliver comprehensive and integrated responses to countries at risk, in protracted crisis and post-crisis situations", including by sharing data, joint analysis and assessment of needs, and "aligned multi-year planning". The UN-World Bank Fragility and Conflict Partnership Trust Fund supports implementation of the initiative, which is described in more detail at https://www.worldbank.org/en/topic/fragilityconflictviolence/brief/the-humanitarian-development-peace-initiative.

[3] For further information on the United Nations Sustainable Development Cooperation Framework Guidance, see https://unsdg.un.org/resources/united-nations-sustainable-development-cooperation-framework-guidance.

[4] For more detail, see the 2019 review of efforts by Sweden and the United Kingdom to implement the nexus approach, published by Development Initiatives at https://www.alnap.org/help-library/key-questions-and-considerations-for-donors-at-the-triple-nexus-lessons-from-uk-and. Another overview is the 2019 OECD Peer Review of Sweden at https://dx.doi.org/10.1787/9f83244b-en.

[5] This paragraph reflects findings from a survey of bilateral partners at both headquarters and field level, which INCAF conducted in 2017 to identify programmatic progress in implementing nexus approaches. These findings were presented and discussed at a meeting of the International Association of Professionals in Humanitarian Assistance and Protection in 2018. A recording of the event is available at https://phap.org/PHAP/Events/OEV2018/OEV180911.aspx?EventKey=OEV180911.

2 Progress and bottlenecks in implementing the Nexus Recommendation

The DAC Recommendation on the Humanitarian-Development-Peace Nexus provides a common set of principles "to address risks and vulnerabilities, strengthen prevention efforts and reduce need in order to ensure that we reach the furthest behind". This chapter reviews efforts that adherents have undertaken in alignment with the DAC Recommendation specifically and, more broadly, to implement related policy agendas and commitments since the 2016 World Humanitarian Summit. In the spirit of collective learning, it identifies key outstanding challenges, bottlenecks and opportunities for joint learning. The discussion largely follows the structure of the Recommendation and is organised around its 11 principles across the dimensions of better co-ordination, programming and financing.

As noted in Chapter 1, the World Humanitarian Summit in 2016 provided impetus to the triple nexus approach, with the adoption of the Development Assistance Committee (DAC) Nexus Recommendation" by "Recommendation on the Humanitarian-Development-Peace Nexus in 2019 marking another milestone. This is why, in the spirit of collective learning, this chapter looks at progress and stumbling blocks in complying with the principles of the DAC Recommendation not only in the three years since its adoption, but also over the five years. In the same vein, the chapter focuses on the overall efforts of adherents that align with these principles, whether such efforts are explicitly intended to implement the DAC Recommendation, or they are aligned to other, related policy agendas and commitments such as those under the Grand Bargain.

The chapter is organised in three sections that largely correspond to the 11 principles across three dimensions elaborated in the DAC Recommendation: better co-ordination (principles III.1-III.3); programming (principles IV.1-IV.6); and financing (principles V.1 and V.2). In section 2.4.2 on programming, three principles (IV.2, IV.4 and IV.5) are grouped and discussed under the heading "Linking the nexus with other relevant policy agendas".

2.1. Strengthening co-ordination

Significant progress has been made in recent years in developing new approaches to a shared understanding of how to reduce risks and improve resilience. However, challenges remain, both to make co-ordination work and to ensure that joint analysis and joined-up planning translate into programming.

Making joint context analysis and joined-up planning work

There has been meaningful progress in fostering joined-up context analysis and planning, with widespread piloting of new, promising approaches. These include the adoption of collective outcomes in 24 of the 25 nexus pilot countries (Inter-Agency Standing Committee, 2021[1]); experimentation with new tools and platforms for joint country analysis; knowledge sharing and joint learning through the DAC-United Nations (UN) Dialogue. Still, several outstanding bottlenecks require attention. For example, evidence that international actors are ready and able to meaningfully commit to delivering under one strategy remains patchy. In addition, and despite existing guidance, a common understanding of the concept of collective outcomes is lacking. Finally, how stakeholders assess a particular context and design their planning is not always conducive to joined-up approaches. An area for further policy research is how local actors can be included more meaningfully in joined-up planning processes.

Empowering leadership for cost-effective co-ordination

Leadership and co-ordination models vary greatly across contexts, with contrasting levels of perceived success. Experience in several countries shows there is potential for better nexus co-ordination adapted to the type of context, as discussed in section 3.7 in Chapter 3 on investing in national and local capacities and systems. In general, however, there remains a deficit in leadership and co-ordination. The survey conducted for this report found that, overall, UN Resident Coordinators (RCs) are perceived to be the main providers of nexus leadership and co-ordination across different contexts, ahead of national governments and major donors (Figure 2.1).

Figure 2.1. Who leads and co-ordinates efforts across the nexus?

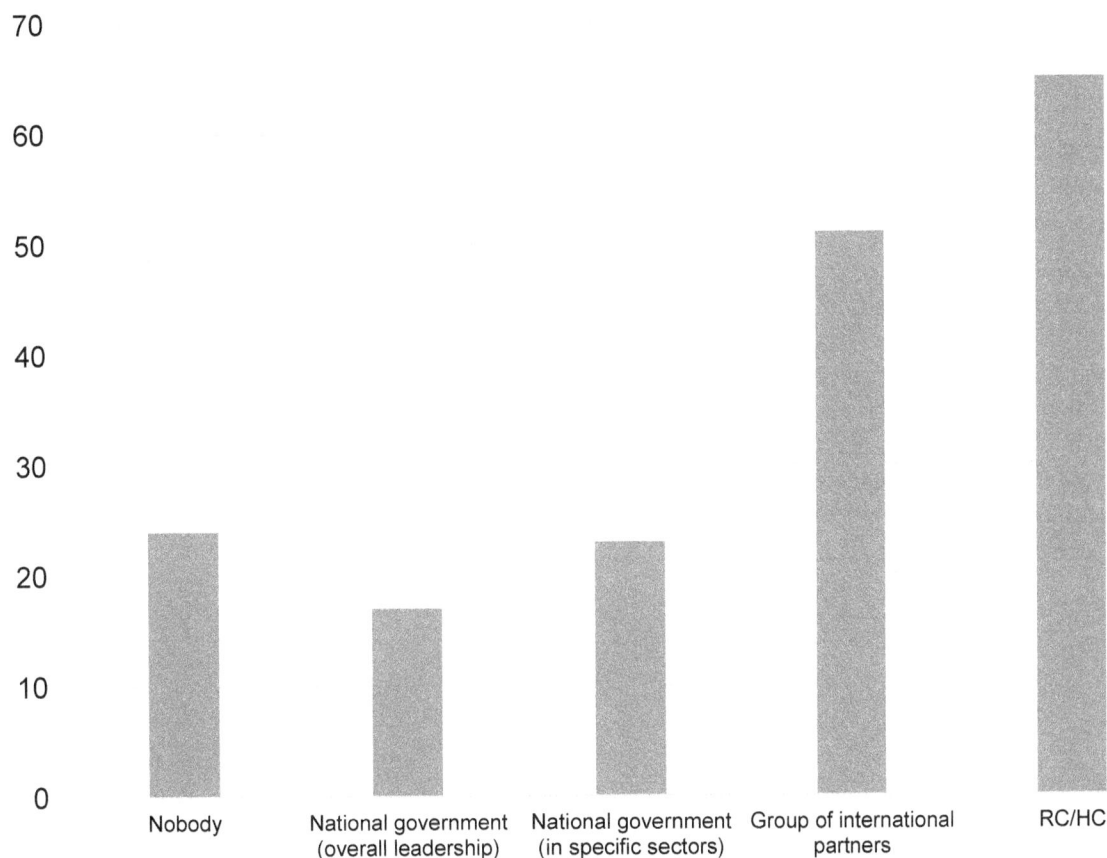

Note: The question in the survey reads: "In your geographic area of responsibility, who leads and co-ordinates the design and implementation of a collective response integrating a nexus approach? (Several answers possible.)"
Source: Nexus Interim Report Survey

Three bottlenecks can be noted. First, improving the ability of national governments to play their role in the nexus approach appears to depend on the degree to which sustainable development challenges are a national priority; the level of trust between government and aid providers; and the resources (capacity, technical expertise and funding) available to support nationally-led co-ordination (OECD, forthcoming[2]; Perret, 2019[3]). Second, while there is much room to support and empower appropriate leadership and co-ordination by UN RCs, in particular those who also serve as Humanitarian Coordinators (HCs) (MOPAN, 2021[4]), this requires clarifying expectations for their role beyond co-ordinating UN and Humanitarian Country Teams and ensuring matching capacity to support the RC/HC functions. Third, in many contexts, donor co-ordination remains a weak point of the nexus co-ordination architecture (OECD, forthcoming[2]). Contexts where a country champion has emerged among bilateral partners to coalesce those partners' efforts offer a useful model that could usefully be replicated more systematically. Two issues require further policy research: first, best practices in the safeguarding of humanitarian principles in complex environments and second, effective incentives for promoting partnerships with multilateral development banks.

Ensuring adequate political engagement

Institutionally, the humanitarian-development-peace nexus approach demands new types of linkages among a diverse set of actors. The role of diplomatic actors deserves to be singled out as their unique mobility across the nexus allows them to draw on their networks and expertise to support sustainable peace and development outcomes in fragile contexts. (Forsberg and Marley, 2020[5]) It is important that governance, diplomatic, stabilisation and civilian security interventions are joined up and coherent with development and peace outcomes and ensure that humanitarian access is protected and that humanitarian principles are respected.

A few noteworthy initiatives have emerged that aim to enhance how diplomatic, stabilisation and civilian security interventions are joined up and coherent with humanitarian, development and peace outcomes (Box 2.1). There is also anecdotal evidence of diplomats and/or political actors mediating solutions and using their political influence to support conflict prevention, humanitarian access and outcomes, peacebuilding, and conflict resolution. Broadly speaking, however, the integration of the peace pillar into the nexus approach remains at a very early stage. This is illustrated by the low response rate to the Nexus Interim Report Survey by peace actors, with only 3% of valid questionnaires attributable to respondents from the peace pillar. Limited nexus literacy and awareness among actors of the peace pillar therefore appears as a key bottleneck.

Box 2.1. Nexus in practice: Country examples of an engaged peace pillar

Concrete examples of good practice demonstrate the strategic benefits of a true triple nexus approach, with meaningful engagement of actors from the peace pillar. Three context-specific examples can serve as models to inspire other nexus approaches:

- In Chad, the HDP Nexus Task Force, created in 2017, brings together bilateral development co-operation providers, development banks and humanitarian donors, allowing enhanced dialogue between humanitarian, development, and peace and security actors. While the co-existence of humanitarian, development and security approaches in unstable areas around Lake Chad requires carefully calibrated operational interactions that help preserve humanitarian space, the enhanced institutional space for strategic dialogue among key partners is a significant development.

- In the West Bank and Gaza Strip, the EU and like-minded donors are enhancing programmatic synergies by expanding the European Joint Strategy to include broader HDP nexus actors such as the UN. The shift was in recognition of the unchanging drivers of vulnerability and humanitarian needs, linked to the broader peace and security context. Nexus-minded programming includes a project focused on community protection and institutional capacity building that targets communities with among the greatest vulnerabilities and risks of displacement and the lowest access to basic services. In 2021, a rapid damage and needs assessment was conducted in the Gaza Strip to promote the building back better approach.

- In Yemen, a World Bank and UN partnership provides an interesting pilot case study in financing nexus priorities. The deployment of a World Bank advisor to support the UN Special Envoy for Yemen between 2014 and 2017 allowed the UN and World Bank to co-ordinate efforts during critical rounds of peace negotiations and in response to the humanitarian crisis. As the crisis deepened, the partnership served as a financing conduit linking the political process to field operations, channelling more than USD 1 billion in World Bank emergency funding through various UN entities to provide community support and help preserve critical institutional capacity. In addition to the availability of financing, the collaboration and support the World Bank provided to existing processes across the nexus in Yemen was an important contribution.

Note: These examples illustrate effective practices in particular contexts and may not necessarily be replicable in other contexts. For Chad and West Bank and Gaza Strip information originates from interviews and unofficial documents consulted by the authors.
Source: Bosire (2018[6]), *The UN-World Bank Partnership in Yemen: Lessons Learned from the Deployment of a UN-World Bank Adviser in the Office of the Special Envoy of the Secretary-General.*

2.2. Strengthening programming

New operational practices reflecting the programming principles of the DAC Recommendation are surfacing across operational contexts. Identifying and scaling up such good practices would require sustained collective investment in joint learning and evidence. There is little visible progress in strengthening transparency and the voice and participation of people affected by crises and fragility.

Prioritising prevention and peacebuilding, investing in development whenever possible

Preliminary evidence suggests that – while the volume of official development assistance (ODA) to peace in fragile contexts has experienced peaks and troughs since 2009 – overall, there has been a gradual increase in the proportion of all donors' ODA to humanitarian needs and a gradual reduction in the proportion going towards development and peace, especially in extremely fragile contexts. This trend varies according to year and recipient country. In extremely fragile contexts, peace ODA is more focused on basic safety and security, while in other fragile contexts, a greater proportion goes to core government functions. Inclusive political processes are a priority across levels of fragility.

Research for this report finds only limited evidence of concrete progress in implementing the DAC Recommendation principle of prioritising prevention and peacebuilding, while investing in development remains most visible in the more stable among fragile contexts. Further attention to this area would be necessary to help inform decision making. Some of the most tangible progress has been made through recent initiatives, within both the DAC and the Inter-Agency Standing Committee frameworks, to identify how to maximise the positive impact of development and humanitarian interventions on peace outcomes.

Enhancing application of conflict sensitivity and do no harm

Despite some progress on enhancing the systematic use of conflict analysis among some actors, the Nexus Interim Report Survey indicates that conflict and political economy analysis are the least-used input to inform planning and programming (Figure 2.2).

Figure 2.2. What types of analysis are used most often as input for planning processes?

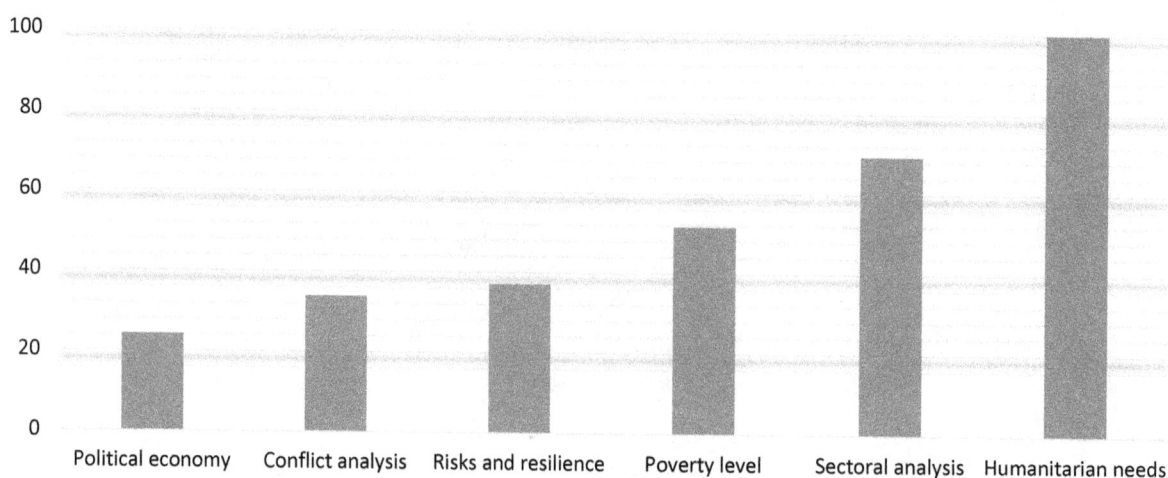

Note: Scores along the vertical axis represent a composite value based on respondents' ranking of most-used to least-used type of input.
Source: Nexus Interim Report Survey.

The situation in Afghanistan has brought into sharper focus the need to understand and measure the impact of ODA on peace outcomes, prompting International Network on Conflict and Fragility (INCAF) and the DAC Network on Development Evaluation to establish a dedicated joint task team. Some work is still needed to design suitable gender analysis methodologies as, to date; gender-sensitive context analysis fails to translate into effective programming. Learning lessons from contexts where collective outcomes have focused on social cohesion and conflict prevention is one area for further policy research.

Investing in learning and evidence

The survey conducted for this report suggests that widespread questions persist about how to assess progress in implementing the nexus, with 48% of respondents indicating that they do not have a way to measure success. Still, an increasing number of DAC members, UN entities and civil society organisations have engaged in evaluating their performance in implementing a nexus approach, often by combining an assessment of impact and internal fitness for purpose. OECD Development Co-operation Peer Reviews and those of the Multilateral Organisation Performance Assessment Network (MOPAN) are additional useful sources of relevant information on individual institutions' performance for the purpose of collective monitoring. Adherents' efforts also include the commission of longitudinal meta-analyses of the response in various contexts, ranging from Afghanistan (Zürcher, 2020[7]) to the Democratic Republic of the Congo (Transition International, 2016[8]). Ultimately, any definition of success must be (co-)owned by the people affected by crises or fragility or their legitimate representatives. Furthermore, existing DAC criteria can be used and adapted to the specificities of implementing the nexus in fragile contexts.

Linking the nexus with other relevant policy agendas

Meaningful progress has occurred on three additional principles of the DAC Recommendation (IV.2, IV.4 and IV.5), though this is related to the implementation of other policy agendas and global commitments. It is important for adherents to be aware of these linkages to ensure synergies in their efforts.

Adopting more people-centred approaches

The humanitarian sector has adopted a people-centred approach as a core professional standard for more than a decade. The development co-operation sector's methodology of community-driven development closely aligns with this operating principle. In both sectors, these approaches are the subject of extensive policy research, guidance and training.

Promoting risk-informed programming

The rich body of policy literature around risk-informed programming in the humanitarian and development sectors has translated into programmatic changes among some DAC and UN adherents. The COVID-19 pandemic — and, more recently, violent political transitions in Afghanistan and several West African countries — have tested international actors' ability to adjust to changes in the operational environment. In addition to anecdotal evidence that actors are responding creatively and with greater agility under extraordinary circumstances, these challenges have prompted many adherents to initiate internal discussions about how to retain their newly won flexibility and further enhance their anticipatory capacity.

Strengthening national and local capacities

There is an opportunity to integrate the localisation agenda into nexus approaches. Currently using national and subnational delivery systems is rarely the default option. Despite positive examples (e.g. in the West Bank and Gaza Strip), efforts to empower domestic non-governmental organisations, the private sector and local government actors in fragile and conflict-affected settings by ensuring they have meaningful roles and responsibilities in project design, implementation and evaluation are still insufficient (Torres and Dela Cruz, 2021[9]). Strengthening national and local capacities is especially important, given their importance for long-term development outcomes (Poole and Culbert, 2019[10]). There is also great potential for international actors to learn from local stakeholders, who often can bridge the nexus pillars in their work and may only demarcate the pillars to fit the international system.

Several recent studies have assessed constraints to shifting a larger share of ODA from intermediaries to local organisations and proposed ways to address the bottlenecks (OECD, forthcoming[11]). However, inclusion and efforts to strengthen local capacities still require more attention. In 2021, the DAC buttressed its normative framework with the adoption of the Recommendation on Enabling Civil Society in Development Co-operation and Humanitarian Assistance.

Integrating a gender focus

Gender equality is fundamental to preventing conflict and fragility and attaining sustainable peace. Women's full, equal and meaningful participation in societies, the economy, disaster risk reduction and peace processes — at all stages and levels of decision making – leads to more inclusive economies and more sustainable peace; inequalities and exclusion, on the other hand, spur conflict and fragility. The DAC Recommendation explicitly links to the international women, peace and security agenda, promoting women's equal opportunities in the economy and equal political representation. Enhancing gender equality and women's empowerment in fragile contexts by protecting the rights of women and girls, and striving for inclusive resilience to natural hazards, are prerequisites for achieving not only the 2030 Agenda for Sustainable Development but also the women, peace and security agenda and the Compact on Women, Peace and Security and Humanitarian Action of the Generation Equality Forum (OECD, 2021[12])

2.3. Financing across the nexus

One of the motivating factors for the DAC Recommendation was the sense that crises — and humanitarian funding requests — were ballooning, with limited financing and programming strategies in place to resolve the issues driving these crises and humanitarian suffering. Across total ODA to fragile contexts, overall there has been a gradual increase in the proportion of all donors' ODA to humanitarian needs and a gradual reduction in the proportion going towards development and peace, especially in extremely fragile contexts. There is also a sense of untapped opportunities, with growing evidence that building resilience and peace is cost-effective, and with a greater diversity and volume of financial resources in many fragile contexts.

Both the UN system and bilateral donors have made significant efforts to adjust their financing practices to support nexus approaches, according to survey data, interviews and peer reviews. In particular, progress has been made on financing instruments, approaches and individual projects, though these are sometimes relatively siloed. Nexus approaches have not yet been fully mainstreamed and normalised, and financing streams tend to not yet work together coherently. The financing strategies envisaged by the DAC Recommendation are still largely missing and will be an important next step to support programming and co-ordination towards prioritised, common goals (OECD, forthcoming[11]).

Harnessing collective financing strategies for coherent action

Reducing the risk of conflict and ending need are not a matter of just spending more, but of spending more strategically. The call for financing strategies across the nexus recognises that prioritisation is both hard and inevitable when needs exceed existing resources and that there is a need to improve how it is done — for instance, by including the international financial institutions (IFIs) as nexus actors alongside bilateral donors, the UN system and humanitarian actors. Steps have been taken, including by the OECD, to develop financing strategy approaches that help bring together analysis and decisions on collective priorities, sources and funds and on strategic programming, building on established methodologies and planning processes.

Yet, the role that financing strategy processes could play in coalescing financing and prioritisation decisions has not yet been realised, and collective outcomes remain driven by multilateral actors rather than being truly inclusive. The majority of survey respondents indicated that they felt their team or organisation had never been involved in developing or aligning to financing strategies that bring coherence across the humanitarian, development and peace pillars. Where respondents said their team or organisation had developed such strategies, the majority of these were developed at the level of the respondent's own organisation or across organisations with a similar mandate. It is rare that the government or actors from other pillars of the nexus are involved. Peace financing constitutes a significant gap: There remains a lack of clarity about the definition and role of peace financing, and none of the (few) respondents who identified with the peace pillar reported having been involved in such a financing strategy.

Making financing more nexus ready

To achieve the programming and co-ordination goals of the DAC Recommendation also requires having the right type of financial resources to deploy. Progress has been made in developing instruments and mechanisms that are nexus ready — that is, they are flexible and predictable, allow for a timely crisis response, and facilitate greater involvement from a broader set of actors. The majority of respondents to the Nexus Interim Report Survey reported that their organisation was able to align financing with activities across the nexus where appropriate (64%); keep unallocated or contingent funding available in case of changing needs (55%); commit an adequate proportion of its resources as multi-year financing (53%); and adjust its financing in response to changes in the context (69%). However, the majority did not think (or was not sure) their organisation had the ability to avoid fragmented, siloed or inappropriately short-term funding (55%) (OECD, forthcoming[11]). Some DAC members deliberately do not have a dedicated humanitarian budget for each country and context and are thus have more flexibility to match funding and programming with needs and risk analysis.

Continued attention is needed to get development and peace financing into the most fragile contexts alongside resources for emergency preparedness and humanitarian response and to ensure that humanitarian assistance is sustained sufficiently to allow development activities to embed (Marley, 2022[13]; OECD, forthcoming[11]). Many crises require humanitarian support over a multi-year time frame, and humanitarian assistance should be programmed and financed with that horizon in mind. As the COVID-19 crisis has demonstrated, not everything urgent is humanitarian and not everything long term is development co-operation: Debt relief, macroeconomic stability or political engagement can be urgent in certain contexts.

Against this backdrop, the expanded role that IFIs are playing across the humanitarian, development and peace nexus should be welcomed. An increased number of IFIs have already started to tailor their work to the needs of fragile contexts, with several development banks and the International Monetary Fund having recently developed or put into effect fragility strategies.[1]

References

Bosire, L. (2018), *The UN-World Bank Partnership in Yemen: Lessons Learned from the Deployment of a UN-World Bank Adviser in the Office of the Special Envoy of the Secretary-General*, Department of Political and Peacebuilding Affairs, United Nations, New York. [6]

Forsberg, E. and J. Marley (2020), "Diplomacy and peace in fragile contexts", *OECD Development Co-operation Working Papers*, No. 77, OECD Publishing, Paris, https://doi.org/10.1787/6a684a4b-en. [5]

Inter-Agency Standing Committee (2021), *Mapping Good Practice in the Implementation of Peace Nexus Approaches: Synthesis Report*, https://interagencystandingcommittee.org/system/files/2021-11/IASC%20Mapping%20of%20Good%20Practice%20in%20the%20Implementation%20of%20Humanitarian-Development%20Peace%20Nexus%20Approaches%2C%20Synthesis%20Report.pdf. [1]

Marley, J. (2022), *Building Support for Reform, Governance and Assistance: Policy and Funding for Security Sectors in Fragile and Conflict-affected Contexts*, United Nations, New York. [13]

MOPAN (2021), *Lessons in Multilateral Effectiveness -- Is This Time Different? UNDS Reform: Progress, Challenges and Opportunities*, Multilateral Organisation Performance Assessment Network (MOPAN), Paris, https://www.mopanonline.org/analysis/items/MOPAN_MLE_UNDSR_Progress_challenges_opportunities_June2021_web.pdf (accessed on 4 September 2021). [4]

OECD (2021), *Gender Equality Across the Humanitarian-Development-Peace Nexus*, Gender Equality Perspectives Series, OECD Development Co-operation Directorate, Paris, https://www.oecd.org/dac/gender-equality-across-the-hdp-nexus-july2021.pdf. [12]

OECD (forthcoming), *Co-ordination across the Humanitarian-Development-Peace Nexus*, OECD Publishing, Paris. [2]

OECD (forthcoming), *Financing Across the Nexus*, OECD Publishing, Paris. [11]

Perret, L. (2019), *Operationalizing the Humanitarian-Development-Peace Nexus: Lessons from Colombia, Mali, Nigeria, Somalia and Turkey*, International Organization for Migration, Geneva, https://publications.iom.int/fr/system/files/pdf/operationalizing_hdpn.pdf (accessed on 15 September 2021). [3]

Poole, L. and V. Culbert (2019), *Financing the Nexus: Gaps and Opportunities from a Field Perspective*, United Nations Development Programme, New York, https://www.undp.org/publications/financing-nexus-gaps-and-opportunities-field-perspective (accessed on 19 September 2021). [10]

Torres, S. and D. Dela Cruz (eds.) (2021), *Localizing the Triple Nexus: A Policy Research on the Humanitarian, Development, and Peace Nexus in Nine Contexts*, CSO Partnership for Development Effectiveness, Quezon City, Philippines, https://csopartnership.org/resource/localizing-the-triple-nexus-policy-research-on-humanitarian-developement-and-peace-nexus-in-9-contexts/?wpdmdl=17681&refresh=61c273ffbd36d1640133631. [9]

Transition International (2016), *Bilan de l'Action Humanitaire en RDC 2006-2016 (internal unpublished document)*. [8]

Zürcher, C. (2020), *Meta-Review of Evaluations of Development Assistance to Afghanistan, 2008-2018 - Chapeau Paper*, Federal Ministry for Economic Cooperation and Development, Bonn, https://www.sicherheitneudenken.de/media/download/variant/198198 (accessed on 22 September 2021). [7]

Notes

[1] On 9 March 2022, the International Monetary Fund (IMF) adopted its Strategy for Fragile and Conflict-Affected States, which identifies enhanced cooperation with development, humanitarian, peace, and security actors a key principle of engagement for the Fund. In this regard, it explicitly refers to the DAC Recommendation. The IMF Strategy can be found here: https://www.imf.org/en/Publications/Policy-Papers/Issues/2022/03/14/The-IMF-Strategy-for-Fragile-and-Conflict-Affected-States-515129

3 The Way Forward

This chapter outlines nine areas where adherents to the DAC Recommendation could focus strategic attention in the future based on the review of progress. These include adopting best-fit co-ordination for every context; implementing inclusive financing strategies; promoting nexus literacy and widening the cadre of nexus-specific profiles; empowering leadership for cost-effective co-ordination; enabling and incentivising behaviour through financing; integrating political engagement into the collective approach; improving prioritisation against the collective outcomes; investing in national and local capacities and systems; using the humanitarian-development-peace nexus as an integrator for other policy priorities; and enlarging the roundtable of stakeholders.

3.1. Adopting best-fit co-ordination in every context

Co-ordination cannot mean the same thing everywhere. While co-ordination is a central and familiar term, there is no shared definition that humanitarian, development and peace (HDP) stakeholders can refer to. Diverging interpretations of co-ordination explain in large part the different expectations and anxieties about the nexus. The appropriate model of co-ordination will need to be collectively determined in a responsive and context-sensitive manner, taking into account the need to preserve humanitarian space in relevant settings (OECD, forthcoming[1]).

Despite investments in various new tools for joint analysis, a common framework is still missing. The general enthusiasm for developing a new generation of collective diagnostic tools has not resolved the lack of clarity about the common choice of tools across contexts or the standardisation of the collective decision-making process. To address this persistent bottleneck, it is necessary to streamline and rationalise the use of various joint diagnostic tools, as the DAC-UN Dialogue has started to through the activities of its "Co-ordination in Countries" work stream. In addition, more discipline in capitalising on what already exists would limit the redundancy of tools and the duplication of analysis exercises.

Collective outcomes can provide useful intermediate targets and benchmarks for a given country or context if more consistently interpreted. Developing collective outcomes that are truly collective, with joined-up approaches to planning and programming agreed by all key stakeholders in a given context would meaningfully advance coherence and complementarity. (OECD, forthcoming[1]).

3.2. Implementing inclusive financing strategies

Even when organisations rigorously establish priorities internally, clearly prioritised strategies have been difficult to achieve collectively in the face of demand for funding that outstrips supply across all pillars of the nexus. Without central, co-ordinated decision-making (OECD, forthcoming[2]; Hövelmann, 2020[3]; Fanning and Fullwood-Thomas, 2019[4]), significant gaps between funding asks and response have become endemic. At the same time, existing financing is not necessarily aligned to collective outcomes and donors express the desire to participate in the dialogue and priority setting process as partners, not merely funders.

Financing across the nexus needs to move away from a traditional fundraising model and towards strategic, coherent partnerships between financing providers and implementers across the three pillars of the HDP nexus. This strategic process should include bilateral and multilateral agencies, as well as international financial institutions (IFIs). While nearly 90% of the DAC's humanitarian aid is channelled through multilateral agencies and non-governmental organisations (NGOs), over 70% of official development assistance for development and peace is channelled through mechanisms other than multilateral agencies and NGOs such as governments and IFIs. (OECD, 2022[5]) Depending on the context, consideration should also be given to resources such as remittances and foreign direct investment flows and to transitioning to government financing over time.

To be most effective, financing strategies should help bring together decisions on joint priorities, sourcing of funds and strategic programming. This creates coherence and reduces friction and wasted personnel resources by ensuring programming is fundable. This allows donors to invest more predictably through a pipeline of well-designed, transformative programmes presenting reasonable chances for success. Yet with few exceptions — for example, the area-based approaches in the Democratic Republic of the Congo (DRC) — collective outcome processes have either not included consideration of financing questions or have left such questions to a second stage, divorced from the determination of programming priorities.

There are existing methodologies that can be tapped into, among them the OECD financing for stability methodology as well as public financial management approaches, integrated national financing frameworks and national strategy processes. The OECD is taking steps to further develop and pilot financing strategies using fragility analysis and financing data to inform key financing and strategy processes. The United Nations (UN) Resident Coordinator (RC) system, UN entities, Bilaterals and IFIs all have a role to play in building broad coalitions around collective outcomes and financing strategies.

3.3. Promoting nexus literacy and widening the cadre of nexus-specific profiles

Enhancing both mutual understanding and information sharing among HDP actors remains a critical challenge to better connecting short-term interventions to peace and development objectives. Improving what can be termed "nexus literacy" across these actors is fundamental to address this challenge.

In addition, in the immediate term, building co-ordination and fostering collaboration will also demand dedicated staff time and focus. At country level, clearly fostering a nexus approach requires more than a side job of a few individuals. Dedicated capacity remains important, at least in the initial phases.

Investing in staff with a specific nexus-focused profile has proven important for catalysing and supporting collective efforts, both within donors and institutions at global level and in co-ordination platforms at country level. The growing number of deployed nexus advisors, as described in Box 3.1, is notable in this regard. Nevertheless, there remains a need to better ensure a match between the ever-increasing need for capacities and the limited pool of deployable candidates.

The newly established Nexus Academy[1], a unique collaboration between bilateral and UN adherents to the DAC Recommendation, has the potential to accelerate the availability of trained capacities. Similarly, other initiatives related to institutional capacity building for the nexus approach are also at the starting block or have been launched to address nexus training needs of various categories of personnel.

Box 3.1. The roles and experience of triple nexus advisors: a review of terms of reference

Different organisations deploy nexus advisors or nexus co-ordinators, as they are sometimes called, in a variety of contexts. Nexus advisors can have an external and/or internal focus, as shown by a review of a sampling of the terms of reference and the experience required for these positions.

Inter-agency role. Triple nexus advisors have been recruited by or seconded in support of UN Resident Coordinators / Humanitarian Coordinators (RC/HCs) to facilitate the development of collective outcomes and a nexus co-ordination architecture in, among other contexts, Cameroon, the Democratic Republic of the Congo, Haiti, South Sudan and Sudan. The descriptions of these positions highlight roles such as convening, facilitating and establishing fit-for-purpose co-ordination mechanisms for the nexus approach; setting HDP priorities; supporting joined-up planning and programming with partners; ensuring inclusion of government, donor, NGO and local actors in HDP priority setting and planning; (Inter-Agency Standing Committee, 2021[6]) and strategic advocacy.

The particular way in which roles and responsibilities are expressed depends of course on the context. In Yemen, for instance, a World Bank-UN advisor to the UN special envoy played such an inter-agency role and provided a triple nexus approach to finance in support of the peace negotiations and for humanitarian challenges. (Bosire, 2018[7]) Elsewhere, different arrangements are used for inter-agency nexus co-ordination. The position of co-ordinator of the Libya nexus working group was created by the World Food Programme and seconded by Switzerland in response to operational nexus co-ordination challenges in southern Libya. (Schreiber et al., 2021[8])

Intra-agency role. Several DAC and UN members as well as other actors have deployed nexus advisors to facilitate and support activities of a more internal nature. These positions are focused primarily on internal programme oversight and policy, on contributing to the integration of resilience at all stages of programming, and on operational oversight of programmes with a strong triple nexus component. For example, the majority of Sida's nexus advisors fit this profile.

Extensive experience generally required. The different terms of reference reviewed featured similar requirements for nexus advisor positions in terms of skills and seniority. These include 7-15 years of experience on average; proven expertise across several pillars of the nexus; and, ideally, experience working in fragile or conflict-affected environments and knowledge of the specific context.

Source: Inter-Agency Standing Committee (2021[6]), *Mapping Good Practice in the Implementation of Peace Nexus Approaches: Synthesis Report*, https://interagencystandingcommittee.org/iasc-mapping-good-practice-implementation-humanitarian-development-peace-nexus-approaches-synthesis; Bosire (2018[7]) , *The UN-World Bank Partnership in Yemen: Lessons Learned from the Deployment of a UN-World Bank Adviser in the Office of the Special Envoy of the Secretary-General*; Schreiber et al. (2021[8]), *Co-ordination, Planning and Financing for Development in Libya: Findings and Recommendations of the Joint OECD-UN Mission* (unpublished).

3.4. Empowering leadership for cost-effective co-ordination

Ensuring appropriate resourcing to empower leadership for cost-effective co-ordination remains a challenge. DAC adherents can do more to jointly support the existing co-ordination architecture and identify the best-fit leadership in every context.

The DAC Recommendation recognises the primary responsibility of the state for shaping the path of a country or context towards peace, popular well-being and sustainable development as well as the role that affected societies and local communities play in achieving collective outcomes. The Recommendation further supports a central role for national governments in terms of co-ordination and leadership of the nexus and, over time, financing responsibilities. In practice, the government role in nexus approaches varies, given that states also are not institutionally static and comprise multiple parts and complex relationships. A good HDP nexus implementation starts with tailored approaches that take into account national, subnational and institutional realities and bolster the active engagement of legitimate national stakeholders across society.

Expectations regarding the co-ordination role of the UN RC/HC should be made clear and backed up with adequate staffing and resources. The RC/HC function, supported by RCOs and OCHA, comes out of the Nexus Interim Report Survey and other recent studies (Inter-Agency Standing Committee, 2021[6]) as an important element of the HDP nexus co-ordination architecture. The DAC Recommendation explicitly calls on adherents to financially and politically support and empower appropriate UN leadership to enable this leadership to provide cost-effective co-ordination across the humanitarian, development and peace architecture. There is an identified need to ensure that suitable, strong leaders are appointed to RC/HC positions in fragile contexts and that expectations of these roles are commensurate with political capital and resources available to them (MOPAN, 2021[9]; UN, 2021[10]; Ryan, 2021[11]).

The usefulness of an empowered leadership model referred to in the DAC Recommendation can also apply to other actors who have convening power in a given context, such as diplomats, national co-ordinators and political leaders.

3.5. Enabling and incentivising behaviour through financing

Significant progress has been made to develop financing instruments, approaches and projects such as pooled funds, resilience funds, flexible mid-year funding allocations and long-term framework agreements for trusted implementing partners. However, financing also plays a strategic role, intentional or not, as a tool to enable and incentivise behaviour. How donors allocate funds as well as where they spend these will play a large part in the successful implementation of a nexus approach — for example, in how the fundraising industry approaches crises, in any fragmentation of pitches and competition for funds, and in how successfully implementers maintain focus on sustaining longer-term development approaches.

Some bilateral and multilateral agencies have reviewed or are reviewing their policies and processes to enhance the agility, predictability and coherence of their financing arrangements and reduce the sometimes-negative impacts of competition. INCAF members have found that while some structures and policies need to be adjusted, it is often culture and political economy rather than hard barriers that need to be addressed (OECD, forthcoming[2]).

Shifting these incentives requires a mix of staff expertise, proper institutional set-up and policy permission space, with targeted seed money playing a supporting role to encourage flexibility and collaboration. It is important that such incentives are seen as one part of a broader approach, rather than as specifically fundraising for the nexus. It is also important to address the political economy and narrative. This may include, for example, managing the tension between promoting flexible core funding and measuring so-called nexus financing; exploring how leaders can incentivise staff to use flexibilities that may already exist; and communicating around effectiveness, waste and accountability so that portfolio impact is seen as a key metric rather than solely transactional controls or incentives to disburse.

3.6. Integrating political engagement into the collective approach

Supporting change in partner countries is a political project. In this regard, the alignment of development co-operation and peace is the real breakthrough of the DAC Recommendation. However, political engagement and other tools, instruments and approaches remain underutilised resources in joined-up efforts across the nexus to prevent crises, resolve conflicts and build peace.

The response to humanitarian crises is not only development but also sustainable peace. Without peace, humanitarian needs will not decrease, and development objectives cannot be reached. Addressing the main drivers of crises is a generational endeavour that goes well beyond programming cycles. As a result, development co-operation in and of itself is not enough to create the domestic conditions to reach the Sustainable Development Goals. Development programmes cannot be expected to reduce humanitarian needs durably until a conducive environment is created for development gains to hold and be preserved. The DAC Recommendation recognises that political engagement and diplomacy play a role, alongside development co-operation, in reaching sustainable peace, while humanitarian assistance focuses on people's most critical needs.

The peace element in the HDP nexus is a reminder that the international community engages in contexts of conflict or rising tension to help reach a sustainable peace. Diplomatic and local mediation actors have unique mobility across the HDP nexus and can draw on their networks and skills to support sustainable peace, including by mobilising conflict-sensitive development co-operation in fragile contexts (OECD, 2020[12]). Yet, peace entails many different types of activities and mandates, and there are different understandings of what actually contributes to peace, including security operations (Barakat and Milton, 2020[13]). Real effort to enhance shared understanding among different stakeholders remains necessary.

3.7. Investing in national and local capacities and systems

Investing in national and local capacities and systems cannot be an afterthought (OECD, forthcoming[1]). Collective support and optimal use of public delivery systems for basic social services at national and local level must remain a priority, even in times of crisis. Development co-operation is not the extension of humanitarian assistance. Both urgent and longer-term actions are required in fragile or crisis contexts. Yet, humanitarian actors often become involved in social or physical infrastructure in the absence of alternatives. Those alternatives are traditionally linked to development co-operation. Not only do they require domestic government buy-in and sustainable resources, which can be challenging in fragile contexts; they also require considerable time for implementation.

As a result, international engagement in crisis contexts is over-reliant on extended humanitarian assistance mechanisms even when development co-operation principles could apply. There are still very few existing development mechanisms that are really fit for fragility. Some DAC members, among them Germany, have demonstrated that transitional development assistance and targeted peace interventions can be fit for fragility and provide structural support at local or national level. Those mechanisms can be powerful tools towards peace and recovery when designed as early development instruments rather than extended humanitarian assistance instruments.

Beyond the programming realm, there is also a need to include the stakeholders closest to the affected communities in a more meaningful way in joint analysis and planning processes, in particular local actors and national and international civil society organisations involved in implementing programmes.

3.8. Using the HDP nexus as an integrator for other policy priorities

The HDP nexus should integrate gender equality, climate change and other relevant considerations. It should not become a new, siloed policy area. The nexus approach can help enhance understanding of the interrelationships among various thematic perspectives and improve their coherence in addressing risks and vulnerabilities. For example, recent research by International Network on Conflict and Fragility (INCAF) and the DAC Network on Gender Equality on the articulation of gender across the triple nexus shows the value of a gender lens for nexus approaches (OECD, 2021[14]). In a similar fashion, the nexus approach can help address climate change (Daroca Oller, 2020[15]) — for instance, approaching climate change as a risk multiplier in the fragility landscape and linking frameworks for prevention, disaster response and fragility. Decentralisation of competencies and resources in partner countries to subnational governments can also provide the institutional footing for area-based nexus approaches, as the local level is "a natural place for working beyond silos" (Barakat and Milton, 2020[13]).

3.9. Enlarging the roundtable of stakeholders

The HDP nexus approach has largely developed organically, and the DAC Recommendation provides an opportunity to set clear and measurable system-wide expectations. At both country and global levels, the most successful models have been largely driven by self-selecting coalitions of willing individuals and institutions that identify specific, practical opportunities. This is the obvious and best place to start; as such, opportunities allow approaches to be tested before moving to scale. It is now time for engagement by a wider set of actors and resources, particularly beyond the UN system.

The success of the DAC Recommendation hinges on the important role of additional stakeholders beyond its adherents. Global nexus co-ordination efforts have thus far gravitated towards the UN system, linking in particular to initiatives around UN development reforms and the New Way of Working. However, with 75% of development assistance to extremely fragile contexts being channelled bilaterally, relying on an UN-centric model might rapidly lead to partial implementation of a nexus approach. (OECD, 2022[5])

Multilateral development banks are playing a growing role across the nexus in fragile and conflict-affected settings (Poole and Culbert, 2019[16]). Both loans and grants have been increasing, particularly with the engagement of the International Monetary Fund, the World Bank and regional banks such as the African Development Bank. However, their co-ordination and linkages with other development actors are not always consistent and need to be strengthened.

References

Barakat, S. and S. Milton (2020), "Localisation across the humanitarian-development-peace nexus", *Journal of Peacebuilding and Development*, Vol. 15/2, pp. 147-163, https://doi.org/10.1177/1542316620922805.
[13]

Bosire, L. (2018), *The UN-World Bank Partnership in Yemen: Lessons Learned from the Deployment of a UN-World Bank Adviser in the Office of the Special Envoy of the Secretary-General*, Department of Political and Peacebuilding Affairs, United Nations, New York.
[7]

Daroca Oller, S. (2020), *Exploring the Pathways from Climate-related Risks to Conflict and the Humanitarian-Development-Peace Nexus as an Integrated Response: Guatemala Case Study*, Folke Bernadotte Academy/United Nations Development Programme, Stockholm/New York.
[15]

Fanning, E. and J. Fullwood-Thomas (2019), *The Humanitarian-Development-Peace Nexus: What Does It Mean for Multi-Mandated Organizations?*, Oxfam, Oxford, UK, https://policy-practice.oxfam.org/resources/the-humanitarian-development-peace-nexus-what-does-it-mean-for-multi-mandated-o-620820/.
[4]

Hövelmann, S. (2020), *Triple Nexus to Go*, Centre for Humanitarian Action, Berlin, https://www.chaberlin.org/wp-content/uploads/2020/03/2020-03-triple-nexus-to-go-hoevelmann-en-online.pdf (accessed on 22 June 2021).
[3]

Inter-Agency Standing Committee (2021), *Mapping Good Practice in the Implementation of Peace Nexus Approaches: Synthesis Report*, https://interagencystandingcommittee.org/system/files/2021-11/IASC%20Mapping%20of%20Good%20Practice%20in%20the%20Implementation%20of%20Humanitarian-Development%20Peace%20Nexus%20Approaches%2C%20Synthesis%20Report.pdf.
[6]

MOPAN (2021), *Lessons in Multilateral Effectiveness -- Is This Time Different? UNDS Reform: Progress, Challenges and Opportunities*, Multilateral Organisation Performance Assessment Network (MOPAN), Paris, https://www.mopanonline.org/analysis/items/MOPAN_MLE_UNDSR_Progress_challenges_opportunities_June2021_web.pdf (accessed on 4 September 2021).
[9]

OECD (2022), *Creditor Reporting System (CRS)*, OECD International Development Statistics (database), https://stats.oecd.org/Index.aspx?DataSetCode=crs1 (accessed on 28 April 2022).
[5]

OECD (2021), *Gender Equality Across the Humanitarian-Development-Peace Nexus*, OECD Development Co-operation Directorate, Paris, https://www.oecd.org/dac/gender-equality-across-the-hdp-nexus-july2021.pdf.
[14]

OECD (2020), *States of Fragility 2020*, OECD Publishing, Paris, https://doi.org/10.1787/ba7c22e7-en.
[12]

OECD (forthcoming), *Co-ordination across the Humanitarian-Development-Peace Nexus*, OECD Publishing, Paris.
[1]

OECD (forthcoming), *Financing Across the Nexus*, OECD Publishing, Paris.
[2]

Poole, L. and V. Culbert (2019), *Financing the Nexus: Gaps and Opportunities from a Field Perspective*, United Nations Development Programme, New York, https://www.undp.org/publications/financing-nexus-gaps-and-opportunities-field-perspective (accessed on 19 September 2021).   [16]

Ryan, J. (2021), *Review of UN Integration: Final Report*, United Nations, New York.   [11]

Schreiber, D. et al. (2021), *Co-ordination, Planning and Financing for Development in Libya: Findings and Recommendations of the Joint OECD-UN Mission (unpublished)*, OECD Publishing/United Nations, Paris/New York.   [8]

UN (2021), *Review of the Functioning of the Resident Coordinator System: Rising to the Challenge and Keeping the Promise of the 2030 Agenda for Sustainable Development - Report of the Secretary-General*, https://digitallibrary.un.org/record/3930790?ln=en (accessed on 19 September 2021).   [10]

Notes

[1] The Nexus Academy facilitates joint learning and knowledge exchange to accelerate nexus approaches and promote complementary humanitarian, development and peace actions that tackle the root causes of crises and end need. It is an initiative of the DAC-UN Dialogue, delivered as a common good by UNDP SURGE Academy.

www.ingramcontent.com/pod-product-compliance
Lightning Source LLC
Chambersburg PA
CBHW051234200326
41519CB00025B/7377

9 789264 420496